BURIED BENEATH CLEVELAND

LOST CEMETERIES OF CUYAHOGA COUNTY

WILLIAM G. KREJCI

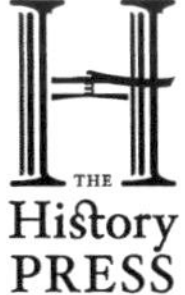

Published by The History Press
Charleston, SC 29403
www.historypress.net

First published 2015

Manufactured in the United States

ISBN 978.1.46711.772.2

Library of Congress Control Number: 2015949906

Notice: The information in this book is true and complete to the best of our knowledge. It is offered without guarantee on the part of the author or The History Press. The author and The History Press disclaim all liability in connection with the use of this book.

CONTENTS

CONTENTS

ACKNOWLEDGEMENTS

Special thanks to the following for their priceless contributions and assistance: Jack Nickels, the Rocky River Historical Society; Louise Varisco, the Strongsville Historical Village; George and Mary Krejci, Chad Thomas, John Nanovsky, Matthew Rump, Ryan McCarbery, Patricia Mahon, Rebecca E. Haaga, Amanda Francazio and Greg Palumbo, the Lakewood Historical Society; Paul Nelson, the Western Reserve Fire Museum and Education Center; Gayle Hill and Charles Cassady Jr., the Western Reserve Historical Society; Ware Petznick, the Shaker Historical Society; Marcia Anselmo, the Gates Mills Historical Society; Roy Larick and Dave Lawrence, the Euclid Historical Museum; the Cleveland Public Library; Cleveland State University; Janet Wood; Lucy Fiore; and Laura Hine.

INTRODUCTION

As we go about our daily lives, we seldom, if ever, wonder what once occupied the places our feet take us. We constantly see things changing before our very eyes. A derelict building might get demolished to make way for a new shopping center. An old farm might be bulldozed and, in a few years, replaced by a modern housing development. A rare sight, however, is the removal of a cemetery. Yet it used to be a common occurrence.

Anyone who has seen the 1982 classic horror film *Poltergeist* knows that it's a bad idea to relocate a cemetery and build on its former site, especially when you leave the bodies behind. First, your chairs begin to move on their own and then a tree almost eats your son. The next thing you know, your five-year-old daughter gets sucked into another dimension through a portal in her bedroom closet. Who needs that kind of a hassle?

All joking aside, what most people don't realize is that moving a cemetery was, at one time, common. When the earliest period of Cleveland's urban sprawl occurred in the 1820s, the need for housing and businesses took precedence over retaining grave sites as hallowed ground. Cemetery movements were inevitable. One thing that is immediately apparent upon seeing where these cemeteries were once located is the fact that most of them exist in what are now the more densely populated parts of the county. This further reinforces the idea that they were moved as a result of urban sprawl. Most small cemeteries that rested farther from the city have been preserved because the land wasn't needed for other purposes.

INTRODUCTION

Cuyahoga County's earliest cemeteries were little more than small, unkempt lots scattered about what would one day become a major metropolitan area. During the 1800s, most urban cemeteries were simply a place for disposing of the dead and weren't treated with much respect. Few were little more than dumping grounds. Before the establishment of township cemeteries, graveyards were, for the most part, small burial plots on family farms that were later opened to neighbors. As farms changed hands, many of these cemeteries became overgrown and were lost.

Many of these grave sites have become parking lots and backyards, with a few scattered about the county in small wooded patches. Some are actually under modern homes and businesses. The question remains whether these are still cemeteries. The answer is a resounding yes. Just because you can't see the headstones doesn't mean that it's not still a graveyard. With the erosion of time, tombstones fall over and settle into the grass. The changing seasons bring leaves down on them, which ultimately turn to mulch and soil. As the years pass, these headstones sink deeper into the earth until they are completely lost from sight and memory. In truth, there usually isn't much left of those who were buried in these cemeteries either, perhaps a few bones here and there.

For the most part, no visible evidence remains of these early burial sites. In some suburban and rural graveyards, small patches of creeping myrtle (*Vinca minor*) can still be found. This hearty plant, native to central and southern Europe, was introduced to North America in the 1700s and was commonly used as a ground cover in these old cemeteries. Though the occasional tombstone fragment might be discovered, this plant is often all that is left to indicate that a site was used as a cemetery.

For those burial grounds that were moved, there was no way for developers to know whether all of the remains had been exhumed. This was primarily due to poor record keeping and the fact that many graves were unmarked—the point being, something is almost always left behind. In some cases, we can only speculate about who was buried in them. Most tombstones are either broken, missing or many inches beneath the surface. What needs to be remembered is that it is still someone's final resting place and should be treated with dignity and respect.

The following pages will reveal the stories and locations of more than fifty cemeteries throughout Cuyahoga County that have been lost to the sands of time. This work is being presented to the public for many reasons, the foremost of these being the proper documentation of these locations for future reference. Should someone happen to be digging on a site and discover human bones, he or she can refer to this work and find an explanation in these pages. Furthermore, this book will tell the stories of those who once occupied this area and ultimately took their repose here. Among them are many veterans of the American Revolution, the War of 1812 and the Civil War. Some were dignitaries and famous scientists while other were people simply trying to carve out a future for their families. In all cases, their stories are fantastic and should be shared. It is also the hope that these historical sites will now be recognized for what they truly are and will one day be surveyed, documented and preserved as such. Keeping that in

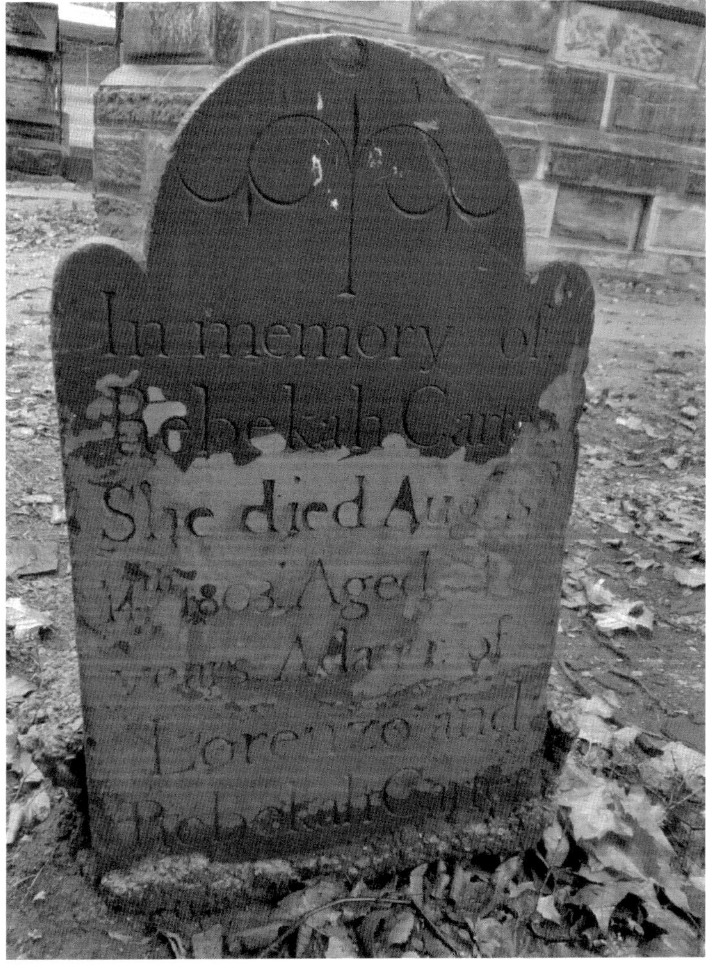

The headstone of three-year-old Rebekah Carter, who died on August 14, 1803, is the oldest in Cuyahoga County. *Author's collection.*

mind, should anyone decide to visit any of these sites, it is strongly advised that anything found there be left as it is. After all, these cemeteries have been desecrated enough, and any trace evidence that remains should be left for professionals to document and future generations to view. Take pictures and leave only footprints.

For your safety and benefit, these sites have been broken up into four classifications. The first of these is *Fully Accessible*. These are sites that sit on public land and can be easily visited with little or no safety hazard. The second class is *Partially Accessible*. These sites share their location with both public and private property. An example of this would be a site that is now occupied by a road as well as a front yard. The public side of these locations may be visited while the part that rests on private property is off limits without permission from the property owner. Next is the classification of *Accessible with Caution*. This includes sites that sit on public property, but their accessibility may be difficult due to issues such as rough terrain, tripping and falling hazards and dangerous plants like poison ivy and wild thorn bushes. Other hazards here could include the frequent presence of aggressive wild animals, hornets, ticks and chiggers. Finally, we come to the last classification: *Strictly Off Limits*. These locations sit entirely on, or are surrounded by, private property and are completely inaccessible to the public. While you may be tempted to visit some of them, please bear in mind that they may be in someone's yard, and trespassing is not encouraged or condoned. Going against these advisories is not in keeping with the true spirit of this work. So, adventurers be warned but have fun exploring the lost cemeteries of Cuyahoga County.

PART I

NORTHEAST CEMETERIES

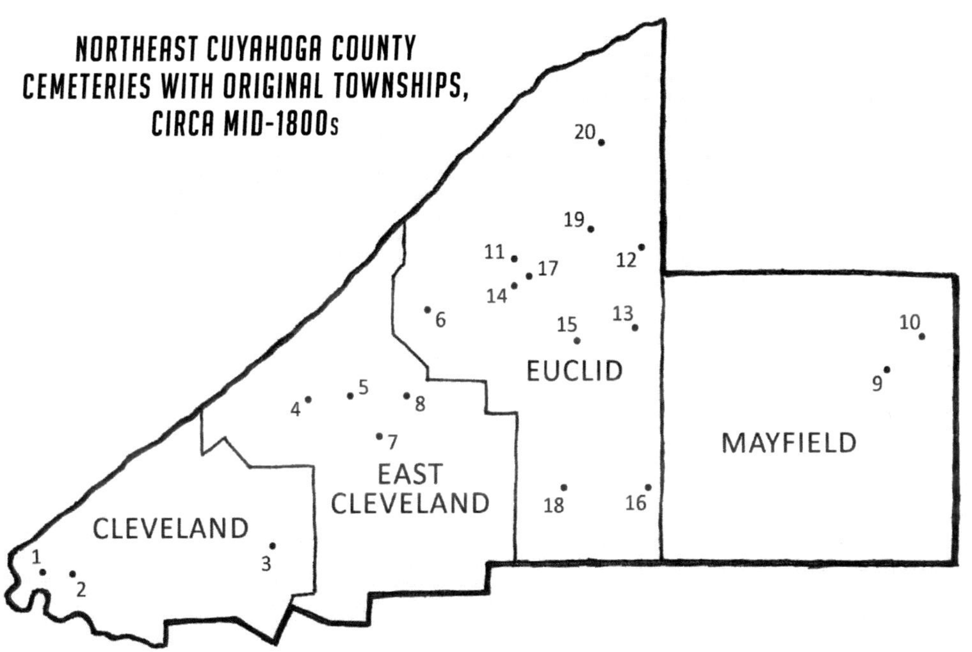

1. Ontario Street Burying Ground
2. Erie Street Cemetery (Partial)
3. Doan's Corners Cemetery
4. Old Glenville Cemetery
5. Hungarian Congregational Church Cemetery
6. Day Family Burying Ground
7. Lewis Family Cemetery
8. Saint Paul's Protestant Episcopal Churchyard
9. Demaline Cemetery
10. Battles Cemetery
11. Euclid Stop 8 Cemetery
12. Peters Farm Cemetery
13. Richmond Cemetery
14. Crosier Cemetery
15. Spring Family Cemetery
16. Silas Johnson Family Cemetery
17. Bliss Cemetery
18. Kellogg Family Cemetery
19. Payne Family Cemetery
20. Johnson/DeVoe Family Cemetery

1
ONTARIO STREET BURYING GROUND

URBAN SPRAWL

Lat 41°29'52.836" N, long 81°41'29.854" W
41.498010, -81.691626
Status: Fully Accessible

As with any story, it's always best to start at the beginning. The official start to this story commences with the founding of the Ontario Street Burying Ground in Cleveland. This cemetery was located just south of Public Square, on what is now the corner of Ontario and Prospect Avenues. Beginning at the northeast corner of this intersection, it ran south along the eastern side of Ontario Avenue to Huron Road. Prospect Avenue, not added as a street until 1831, now cuts through what was the northern end of this cemetery.

The first burial here was a twenty-three-year-old man named David Eldridge, who drowned while crossing the Grand River on June 3, 1797, and was brought to Cleveland the next day for burial. Eldridge was an employee of surveyor Amzi Atwater and was bringing a land party, which included the Carter family, west from Conneaut to Cleveland. It was on Sunday, June 4, that the site for this cemetery was selected. It is recorded that Corinthians 15 was read at the burial service. The plot was originally chosen at the north end of surveyed lots ninety-seven and ninety-eight, but over time, the cemetery expanded southward. Eldridge is believed to be the first European American buried in the city of Cleveland.

The second burial was that of Peleg Washburn, an apprentice to blacksmith Nathaniel Doan, who died on August 6, 1797, of dysentery.

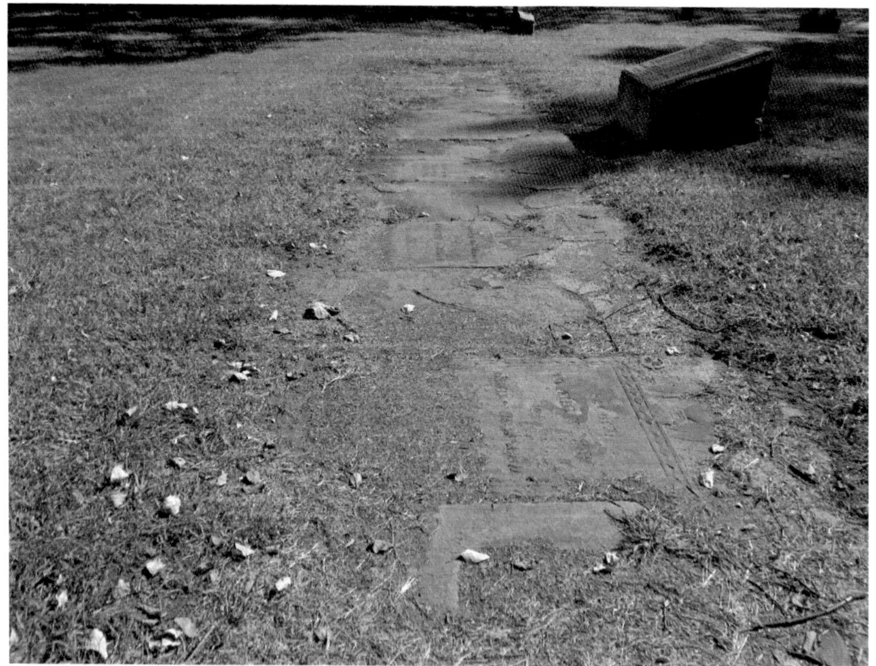

The concrete slab at Erie Street Cemetery containing the headstones moved from the Ontario Street Burying Ground. *Author's collection.*

William Andrews, a surveyor's flagman, was the third to be interred here. His death occurred on September 7 of that same year, with his burial taking place the following day.

Of the eighteen deaths in Cleveland between 1797 and 1808, eleven were from drowning. Some form of swamp fever, ague or malaria caused nearly all the others.

In 1825, as the population of Cleveland was expanded and land near the center of town became more valuable, Hiram Hunt, the owner of lots ninety-seven and ninety-eight, expressed a desire to build on the site of the Ontario Street Burying Ground. Thus, in 1826, Leonard Case Sr. purchased just over ten acres on the outskirts of the village and turned the land over for the cost of one dollar for the expressed use of a cemetery. That year, the remains of nearly three hundred early Cleveland residents were moved from Ontario Street to the new Erie Street Cemetery. Ten years later, construction workers located many bones on the former site of the cemetery. There's no telling how many remains still lie beneath Prospect Avenue and the surrounding area.

The oldest tombstone that survives from this cemetery is that of Rebekah Carter, the three-year-old daughter of Major Lorenzo Carter, who died on August 14, 1803. Hers is the oldest known headstone in Cuyahoga County. There is also a newer stone marking the grave of David Eldridge in section three of lot forty-three. Many of these reburials from the Ontario Street Burying Ground can be located throughout sections one and seven near the East 9th Street entrance. Also found here is a concrete slab that contains the headstones of sixteen early settlers who died between 1805 and 1824. Among them is the headstone for thirty-nine-year-old Eliakim Nash, who died on December 28, 1812. This is the oldest marker in the county to bear a Masonic insignia.

2
ERIE STREET CEMETERY (PARTIAL)

NOT AS CROWDED AS IT ONCE WAS

Lat 41°29'49.391" N, long 81°41'00.229" W
41.497053, -81.683397
Status: Fully Accessible

As previously mentioned, Erie Street Cemetery was opened in 1826, when Leonard Case Sr. donated two acres of his own land and spent forty-five dollars for an additional eight acres adjoining, which were owned by Charles Douglas and William Eldridge. The town's infirmary was already situated on this second section. Supposedly mentioned within the purchasing agreement was a clause that the land would be used expressly as a cemetery or it would revert back to the original owners. This clause would haunt Cleveland officials for many years to come.

While the task of moving the graves from Ontario Street was underway, the city also decided to erect a poorhouse and a gunpowder warehouse at the east end of the property. When Douglas received word of these additions, he sued the city. He ultimately settled out of court and was paid $3,300.

The first new burial at Erie Street was Minerva M. White, the infant daughter of Moses and Mary White, in September 1827. Many other notables were buried here as well, including James Kingsbury, John Malvin, Leonard Case and John Willey. Joc-O-Sot, said to be a great Sauk chief, died in Cleveland in 1844 and was buried close to the main drive that bisects the cemetery. In truth, Joc-O-Sot was not a chief. At thirty-four years old, he was too young.

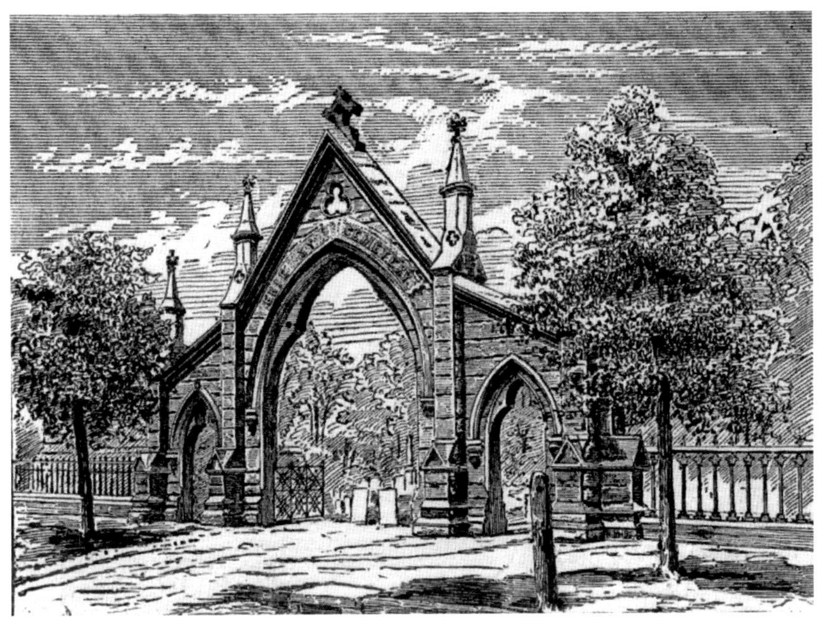

Erie Street Cemetery entrance, circa 1876. *Cleveland State University. Michael Schwartz Library.*

In 1837, the city poorhouse at the east end became the city hospital and was consolidated with the old infirmary. Three years later, the cemetery was officially laid out into individual lots, and a record of burials was established. Erie Street Cemetery, or so everyone hoped, would no longer be a general dumping ground for dead bodies. Among these newly laid out lots was a small section reserved for Roman Catholics, the first in the area, which predates the first Catholic cemetery by more than ten years. In 1851, the city hospital was finally torn down to make room for more burials.

In 1870, a high iron fence was erected around the cemetery to replace the old wooden fence that encompassed the grounds. The fence cost $4,000. The following year, the grand sandstone entryway was built at the cost of $8,296.

With all this time and money being put into the Erie Street Cemetery, one would think that its existence would be secure. However, this was not the case. In September 1884, the cemetery was deemed "unhealthy" and a hazard to the city. A proposal was put forth to have it relocated to either Woodland Cemetery or to a new potter's field. This statement coincided with a proposal to erect a new market house, certainly not a coincidence. The cemetery showed its profitability, and the plan to move the burial ground was abandoned, at least for the time being. Furthermore, it was pointed out that if the cemetery were moved, the land would revert back to the Case and Douglas families.

The cemetery was clearly making money. For a number of years, fresh soil was brought in and dumped on top of the older sections, which allowed the city to make money off of new burials on top of previous ones. Some graves were actually being buried only three feet deep. Still, the land on which the cemetery sat was proving to be more valuable than the income from burials.

By 1897, the city council was looking to take legal action to have the cemetery moved. All it needed was to find a magic loophole that would keep the land from the Case and Douglas families. Despite the constant propositions to relocate the cemetery, burials still took place well into the early twentieth century. In 1901, the cemetery grounds were proposed as a site for the new Cleveland City Hall. It was now estimated that nearly twenty-five thousand bodies were already interred there. The following year, Cleveland city councilman Fred Bellstein proposed the cemetery as a site for the widening of Sumner Street, now just an inconspicuous alley that runs along the southern wall of the cemetery. The city might have been looking at taking possession of the land by ceding it to a right of way or legal highway. None of this was necessary, and it wasn't long before another answer was found. On closer examination of the title transfers, the city learned that nowhere did it state that the land would revert back to the original owners. This new information allowed the city to begin the process of vacating Erie Street Cemetery.

In 1905, lot owners exchanged their titles to the lots in the cemetery for new lots at the recently opened Highland Park Cemetery. Exhumations began on October 3 of that year, with the first five bodies being exhumed and relocated to Highland Park. By 1912, plans had been revisited to convert the site into a central market. Nearly half of those originally interred were now moved to Highland Park Cemetery. Ten years later, the City of Cleveland looked at converting the old burial ground into a park and playground. The idea was not a new one, as it had been looked at earlier in 1903.

With plans for the new Lorain-Carnegie Avenue Bridge underway in 1925, a proposal was put forth to send Carnegie through the old cemetery grounds. However, an alternate plan was proposed to route the thoroughfare to the south and rededicate the Erie Street Cemetery, as it was turning one hundred. This plan took an additional fifteen years to be realized. But on July 21, 1940, the Western Reserve Early Settler's Association rededicated the cemetery, and it was saved from future defilement. Other contributors to the project were the city planning commission and the WPA.

Sadly, the damage to Erie Street Cemetery has been done, and those historical gravestones that once marked the resting places of some of Cleveland's earliest settlers are gone.

3

DOAN'S CORNERS CEMETERY

THE LITTLE CEMETERY ON EUCLID AVENUE

Lat 41°30'16.919" N, long 81°36'55.796" W
41.504700, -81.615499
Status: Fully Accessible

Doan's Corners once existed as a little community on the corner of Euclid Avenue and Doan Street, which is now East 105th Street. It was named for Nathaniel Doan, who came to Cleveland with the 1797 expedition. That fall, he traveled back to Connecticut with the surveyors and returned to Cleveland with his family the following spring. He opened a blacksmith shop on Superior Avenue, though according to his grandchildren, he never worked as a blacksmith but simply owned the shop. Fever and disease along the Cuyahoga River forced him and his family to move east in 1799 and settle this little community on original lot fourteen in East Cleveland Township.

Doan's Corners Cemetery was officially established on January 9, 1823, but the first burial was that of eighteen-year-old Ann Olivia Baldwin on February 25, 1821. She was the first wife of John Doan, Nathaniel's nephew. Incidentally, at the time of John's death in 1896, he was the oldest man dwelling in Cuyahoga County.

This cemetery was set on a piece of land comprising one acre, purchased from John H. and Elizabeth Strong for forty dollars. The new owner was a cemetery association that divided the back of this acre into thirty-three cemetery lots. Six years later, a second acre was added, as

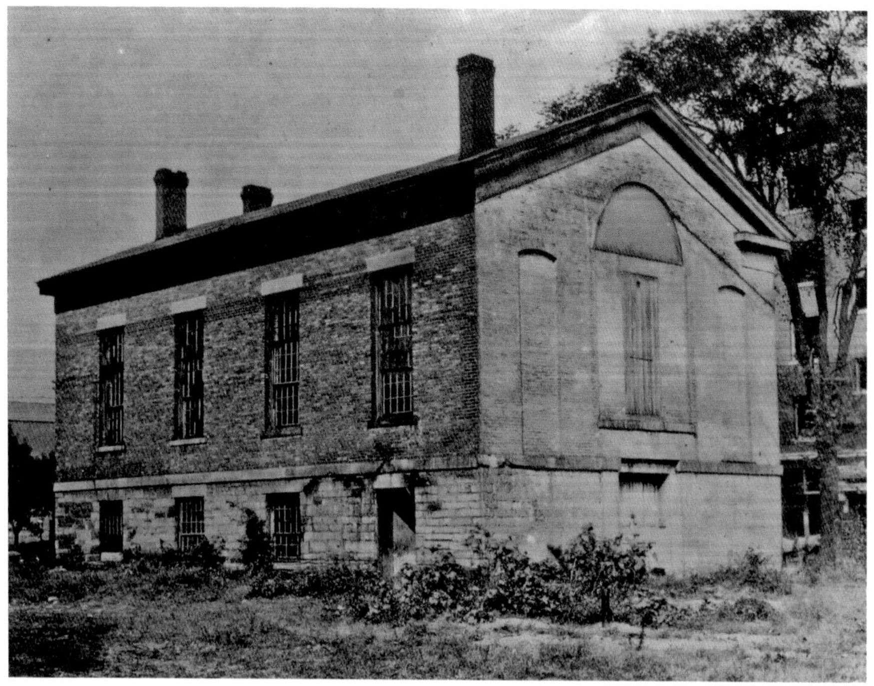

The former Presbyterian church at Doan's Corners circa 1900. The cemetery was located directly behind this structure. *Cleveland Public Library.*

well as a potter's field at the northeast corner. The primary burials here were members of the Doan, Baldwin, Edwards and Strong families.

In 1846, the cemetery association granted the Presbyterian Church permission to build a house of worship on the southeast corner of the lot. It was a simple two-story brick building. This church was used until 1867, when the members of the parish separated from the Presbyterians to form the Euclid Avenue Congregational Church and erected a new building at Euclid and East 96th Street.

Throughout much of the 1870s, the area was used as a public square with the old brick church near the corner and the little cemetery in the back. In 1877, William Halsey Doan converted the old Presbyterian church into an armory. This armory was used as a drill hall for the Euclid Light Infantry. In later years, it became the Forest City Post for the Grand Army of the Republic. The old church building was also used as a carpenter's shop and the Washburn Mission Sunday school.

By 1893, many of the descendants of those buried in the old cemetery began moving the remains of their ancestors to other area cemeteries. Some of the

William Halsey Doan. *Cleveland Public Library.*

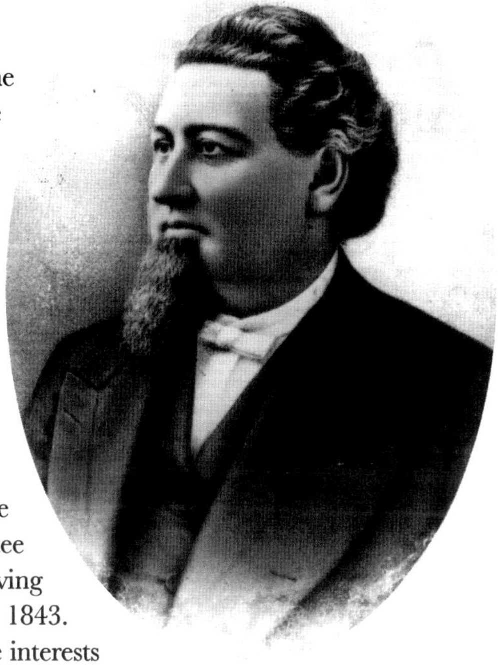

more prominent members of the community were moved to Lake View, but the majority went to the East Cleveland Cemetery.

It was in 1895 that the old cemetery encountered controversy. This happened when the Congregational Church attempted to sell the lot that contained its old church and the cemetery. The problem was it didn't own it. Its sale of the land was contested by George Watkins, the only surviving trustee of the cemetery association, having been elected to that position in 1843. Watkins had since purchased the interests of the cemetery lots from the descendants of the other trustees and was still maintaining what was left of the Doan's Corners Cemetery. Watkins went to court over the matter and produced much evidence to support his claim to the land, including land agreements and burial records that dated back to 1822.

As it turned out, the cemetery association had only leased the land for the church to the congregation. When it relocated to the new church at East 96th and Euclid, the lease was terminated. The church claimed that a tax title amounting to $1,000 it had purchased many years earlier gave it legal rights to the land. Meanwhile, the City of Cleveland took a closer look at the property and learned from records that it was used as a public square, thus giving the city rights to it. A fourth party became involved: E.M. Heisley, who, with his father, had secured quitclaim deeds from cemetery lot owners many years earlier.

It appears that, in the end, all had some right to the land. With the property being as valuable as it was, the cemetery association sold the cemetery land to the Congregational Church in April 1899. By October 1904, the final removal of the marked graves had been started. These belonged to the Edwards family and were relocated to Woodland Cemetery, though no reburial records exist.

One year later, the land was sold to the Cleveland Trust Company for $40,000. That winter, the remainder of the bodies that could be located was moved to the East Cleveland Cemetery. The following spring, the old church was torn down, and a new building, the Alhambra Theatre, was erected in its place. Interestingly, the foundation of the old church had been incorporated into the backstage area of the theater and was visible until the building was demolished in 1976.

Also built in 1906, directly on the northwest corner of East 105th and Euclid (the southeast corner of the lot), was the new bank building for the Cleveland Trust Company. The following year, workmen excavating behind the new bank discovered a set of human remains that had been left behind from the old cemetery. This find was made in the former potter's field. Had there been a tombstone, the grave certainly would have been relocated with the others between 1893 and 1905. As it was, most potter's fields contained no markers.

Today, this property is the location of the Ronald McDonald House on the northwest corner of East 105th and Euclid. The section that specifically contained the cemetery site is now the northern parking lot and eastern entrance to the property.

4

OLD GLENVILLE CEMETERY

OLD AND IN THE WAY

Lat 41°32'26.718" N, long 81°36'23.173" W
41.540755, -81.606437
Status: Fully Accessible

The Old Glenville Cemetery was once located on the south side of the intersection of St. Clair Avenue and East 112th Street. Around 1815, area residents established it on a quarter-acre piece of land, a popular size for burial grounds in the early years. The land belonged to Dr. Smith Inglehart. In its time, it was regarded as one of the most picturesque cemeteries in the area.

In October 1853, Dr. Inglehart sold the cemetery to Horace Gunn, William Morrow, Jeremiah Shumway and William Foster for $16.53 with the understanding that it would be used as a burial ground for the residents of East Cleveland Township School Districts Five and Six. Furthermore, the contract stated that the cemetery was to be free to the public.

By the 1870s, the little cemetery had been filled to capacity and fell into disuse shortly thereafter. In the years that followed, it became abandoned and overgrown. Many people with loved ones interred there decided to have the graves removed to other area cemeteries.

In 1889, the widening of St. Clair Avenue was in progress, and on July 16 of that year, seven graves were disinterred. Two were unknown, one was a woman with the last name Batal and the other four were members of the Houghland family—John Houghland; his wife, Betsey Eddy; and two of their children. After the road widening, the rest of the cemetery was left in peace.

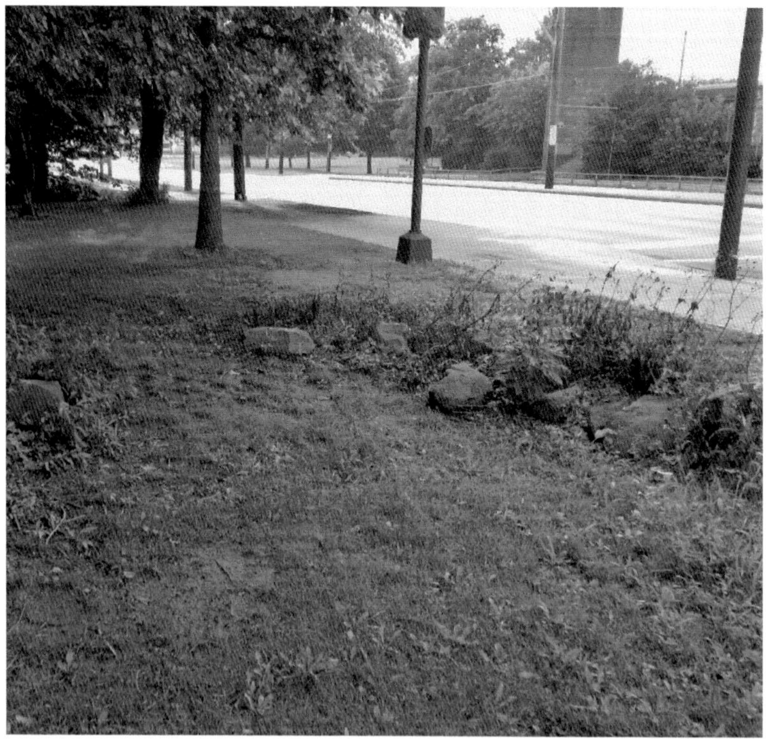

A grassy area at St. Clair Avenue and East 112th Street is all that remains of the Old Glenville Cemetery. *Author's collection.*

By the early 1890s, the cemetery had become so neglected that it was taken over by the state. Within a couple years, it had reverted back to the heirs of Dr. Smith Inglehart, probably due to the fact that it was no longer being actively used as a cemetery and most of the graves had been removed. In 1895, the little cemetery was sold for one dollar to Judge Thomas Kemp Dissette by his son-in-law, one of Dr. Inglehart's heirs. Judge Dissette had lived across the street from the cemetery for years and was expanding his property to the south.

By 1904, only six headstones remained in the Old Glenville Cemetery. It was at this time that Glenville passed an ordinance declaring the cemetery to be a nuisance. Any graves that could be found had to be removed. Thus, the Old Glenville Cemetery was lost forever. Three brick buildings were erected on the front of the site shortly after 1912 but were torn down in the early 1960s to make way for the new Glenville High School. The front of the old cemetery is now a grassy area among a few shady trees. The back is now the northern end of the parking lot for Glenville High School.

5

HUNGARIAN CONGREGATIONAL CHURCH CEMETERY

FIRST B'NAI JESHURUN BURIAL GROUND

Lat 41°32'28.186" N, long 81°35'28.305" W
41.541163, -81.591196
Status: Strictly Off Limits!

This cemetery was established in August 1883 on the western edge of East Cleveland on what was then called Gravel Road. Leopold Berger sold this property to the Hungarian B'nai Jeshurun Congregational Church. In all, it comprised two acres, with the east acre containing a church and the west acre containing the burying ground.

The congregation thrived at the site until 1906, when the Cleveland Short Line Railroad proposed sending its tracks right through the middle of the cemetery. This proposal was fought extensively in court, but ultimately, a jury decided that the Cleveland Short Line would pay the congregation $10,500 in damages to acquire a new burial ground and pay for removing the monuments and bodies to this new cemetery.

Thus, B'nai Jeshurun purchased a five-acre tract immediately to the west, just within the boundaries of the city of Cleveland. This sparked much opposition from neighbors, as no one wanted to see a new cemetery in the area. Regardless, the congregation began moving the graves in December 1906.

Morris Amster, a trustee of the congregation, supervised the work while nine laborers set to the grim task. By mid-February 1907, nearly three

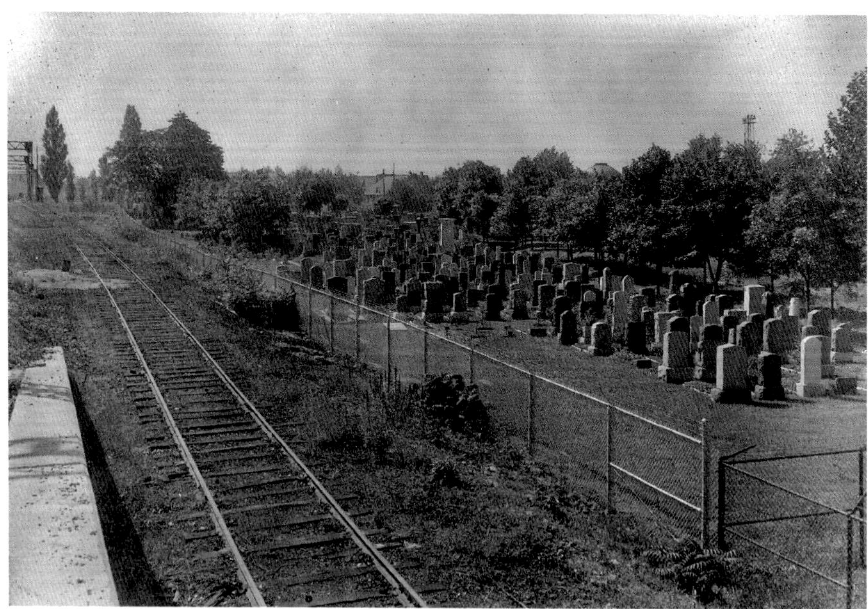

Railroad tracks now occupy the original site of the Hungarian Congregational Church Cemetery. The new cemetery sits just to the west. Photo circa 1930. *Cleveland State University. Michael Schwartz Library.*

hundred bodies had been moved to the new cemetery. The work was completed shortly thereafter.

Today, this new cemetery is known as the Glenville Cemetery at 13009 Shaw Avenue in Cleveland. The congregation demolished the church a few years after the cemetery was removed, relocated farther east and now worships at the Temple on the Heights.

The site of the old cemetery is still a railroad line just north of Shaw Avenue. The embankment is completely weed choked and inaccessible. Furthermore, it lies on private property and is, therefore, strictly off limits.

6
DAY FAMILY BURYING GROUND

EAST 166TH STREET CEMETERY

Lat 41°33'39.413" N, long 81°33'50.572" W
41.560948, -81.564048
Status: Partially Accessible

Travelers down East 166th Street on the outskirts of Cleveland would not suspect that a small family burial ground containing the remains of the Benjamin Day family was once located halfway down this small side street.

Benjamin Day was born on March 24, 1778, in Mendham, Morris County, New Jersey, to Samuel T. Day and Abigail Carter. In 1796, he was married to Nancy Andrews. Soon after, they relocated to Van Buren, Washington County, Pennsylvania, where Benjamin worked as a farmer and distiller. In 1811, he continued on to Cuyahoga County and purchased three hundred acres in what was then Euclid Township. After viewing the land and making certain that it was a sound environment in which to raise a family and prosper, he returned with his family on September 9, 1813. The following afternoon, the newly arrived settlers heard what sounded like thunder off to the west. With no storm approaching, they soon realized it was the sound of cannon fire. What they were hearing was the distant Battle of Lake Erie. Once they realized what they were witnessing, the family was ready to turn around and head back east in the event that the Americans were defeated. A few days later, word arrived of Perry's victory, and the Day family remained on their farm.

This small family cemetery was established around 1840, when Benjamin and Nancy's two-year-old grandson George had passed away. George was the son of Hiram Day and Catherine Beers. Catherine followed her son in 1843. Two years after that, Benjamin and Nancy's twenty-three-year-old daughter Margaret passed. Other interments in this burial ground were Nancy Day in 1861, Benjamin Day in 1872 and Hiram's second wife, Deborah, in 1882.

Following Benjamin's death in 1872, the farm and burial ground passed to his grandson Joseph Addison Day. Over the next thirty years, it was transferred to other family members until it was sold in October 1902 to Charles Johnson. Reserved from this sale was the small quarter-acre burial ground of the Benjamin Day family. Within a year, the property was sold to Ella C. Dorrance, who had plans for laying out a subdivision. The only thing that stood in her way was the Day cemetery. That problem was solved in the spring of 1904, when Dorrance convinced the surviving members of the Day family to sell her the land that was occupied by the cemetery. Subsequently, the graves of Benjamin, Nancy and their daughter Margaret were relocated to Euclid Cemetery on March 28, 1904. Benjamin and Nancy's son, Robert, had purchased a lot at Euclid Cemetery in early 1880 (lot D56) and it was here that his wife, Harriet, was buried in 1881. Robert followed in 1889. A modern monument was placed on this lot following the transfer of the Day family from their original burial site.

Three graves had been removed eight years earlier from the Day Family Burying Ground, those being Hiram Day's two wives and his son, George. This had occurred shortly after Hiram's death in 1896. Those graves were relocated to East Cleveland Cemetery.

Dorrance Avenue was completed in 1905. The following year, the name was altered to East 166th Street. Today, it exists as a small side street that runs north and south between St. Clair Avenue and Wayside Road. The exact location of the old Day Family Burying Ground rests along the western verge of that road. The majority of the cemetery lies beyond the fence beneath a crumbling parking lot just north of a dilapidated structure. This part of the cemetery rests on private property and is not accessible to the public. In any case, no evidence of this ever having been used as a cemetery remains.

7
LEWIS FAMILY CEMETERY

FORGOTTEN AND UNMARKED

Lat 41°31'53.928" N, long 81°34'48.540" W
41.531647, -81.580150
Status: Fully Accessible

This small burial ground was discovered in November 1902 while excavations were being made for the new East Cleveland Baptist Church, located on the southwest corner of Euclid Avenue and Rosemont Road in East Cleveland. When first uncovered, it was suspected to be a Native American burial ground, but speculation was laid to rest when a

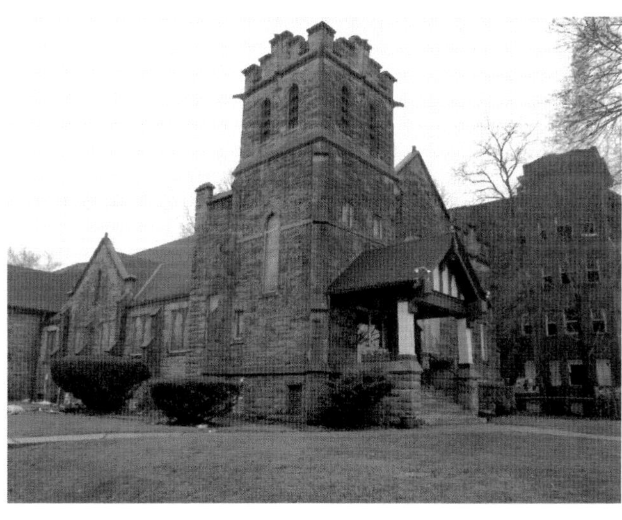

East Cleveland Baptist Church, where graves were unearthed in 1902. *Author's collection.*

coffin was unearthed. The person whose remains were entombed there was never identified; the coffin was dated 1860.

The land that this cemetery once occupied was owned by Chittenden Lewis from July 1856 to December 1864. Chittenden and his wife, Harriet, came to Cleveland from Malone, New York, in 1837. Traveling with them were their four children, a fifth having died back in New York. Two years after their arrival, a sixth child, Elmina Elizabeth Conant Lewis, was born. Four of these children could be accounted for in 1860. The only one missing was Catherine Adelia Lewis, their eldest daughter. Could the found remains be hers?

It is possible that the burial ground was open to neighbors, so there really is no way of knowing whose remains were unearthed or how many other sets of remains are still interred on that small piece of land. Today, this building houses the Starlight Missionary Baptist Church.

8
SAINT PAUL'S PROTESTANT EPISCOPAL CHURCHYARD

COLLAMER VILLAGE

Lat 41°32'31.307" N, long 81°34'13.728" W
41.542030, -81.570480
Status: Fully Accessible

Saint Paul's Protestant Episcopal Congregation was formed in 1843 in what was originally Euclid Village, later called Collamer Village, in East Cleveland Township. On October 22, 1845, John Doane and L.L. Adams, wardens of the congregation, purchased the land for the church and cemetery from area farmers Rodney and Mary Taylor Strong.

Construction on the church began that year but wasn't completed until 1860. The burial ground for this congregation was located on the property adjacent to the back of the church, on the edge of a slight descent to the north, and was shaded by a patch of trees. Though the property didn't enter the hands of the Episcopal Church until 1845, the grounds were used as a cemetery as early as 1830. The first interment was twenty-two-year-old Eliphalet Adams, an uncle of Charles M. Adams, who married one of Rodney and Mary Strong's granddaughters. Another burial that predates the sale of this property to the congregation was that of Sarah, the wife of Johnson Ogram, who died on April 26, 1843.

Though they had sold this land to the church, the Strong family retained interests in the burial ground, the lots, walks, alleys and avenues in particular. In the few years that followed, Rodney and Mary Strong's daughter, Sarah Jane, was married to James Ogram. Two of their children, Frank Strong

Ogram and Mary Elizabeth Ogram, died and were buried there in the early 1850s. Forty-four-year-old Ira C. Sawtell, who had served as overseer of the poor for the city of Cleveland in 1844, also passed during this era. He died of cholera on July 8, 1852. His seventeen-year-old daughter, Elizabeth, followed him to the grave just fourteen days later from the same affliction. Her obituary mourned her as being "much esteemed for her generous qualities…beloved by a large circle of young friends."

Overall, the primary burials in this churchyard were those of the Strong, Ogram, Sawtell, Adams, Van Tine and Foote families.

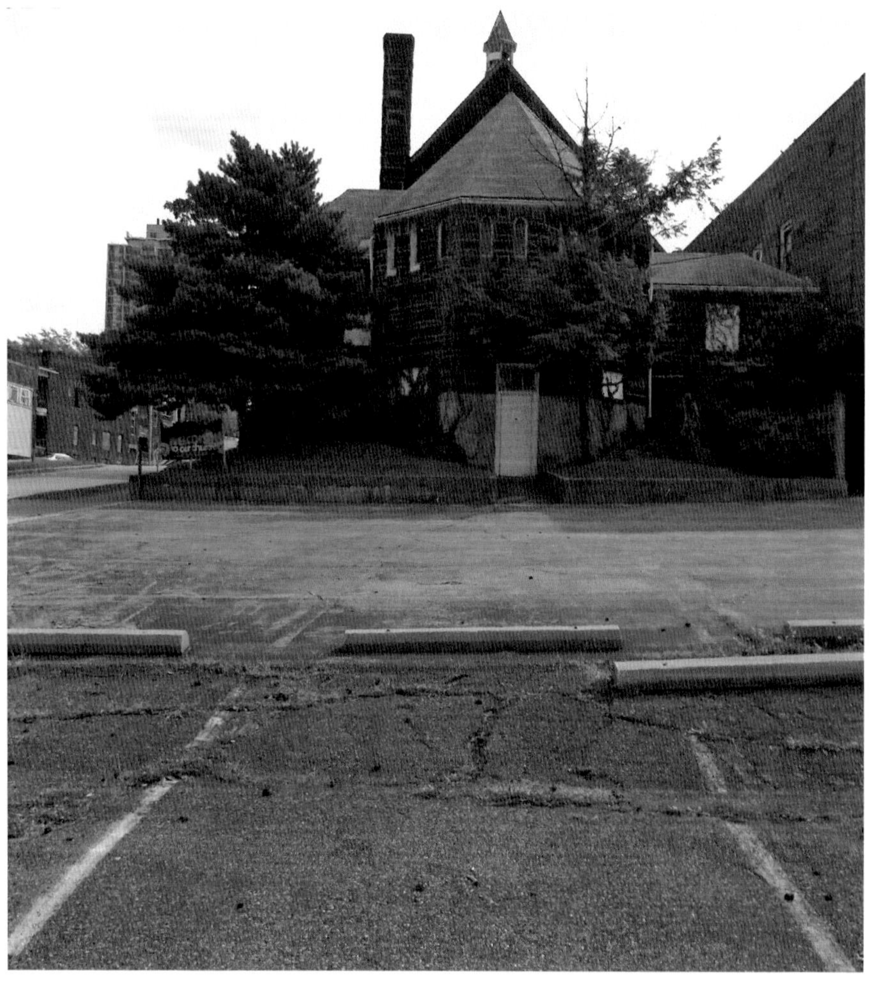

A parking lot and addition to St. Paul's Protestant Episcopal Church now occupy the site of the old burial ground. *Author's collection.*

Mary Taylor Strong passed away on September 28, 1864, and was buried in this cemetery. Her husband followed her to the grave on November 17, 1868. The heirs of Rodney and Mary Strong withdrew their claim on interests in the burial ground in 1895. On April 10 of the following year, Rodney and Mary's remains were relocated to Lake View Cemetery along with their grandchildren, Frank Strong Ogram and Mary Elizabeth Ogram.

By the early 1920s, the old churchyard had fallen into a severe state of neglect, its tombstones now leaning over, and had even been condemned by town authorities some ten years earlier. It was at this time that a three-story school and parish hall were planned on the site of the burying ground. The fact that this section of the graveyard was still occupied delayed the plans. Through legal channels, the parish secured a quitclaim deed from the descendants of those that remained buried in the churchyard. These descendants sold their lots back to the church in 1922 for one dollar and moving costs. The grounds were vacated, and with the exception of those buried in the Sawtell lot (the remains of whom were moved to section forty-two, lot one hundred at Lake View Cemetery), the bodies that could be located were moved to a lot in section two of East Cleveland Cemetery that had been purchased by the parish.

Following the removal of these graves, the land was graded, and construction commenced on the school and parish hall, which were dedicated on January 31, 1923. Today, the property is owned by the Antioch Christian Fellowship Church and is located on the northwest corner of Euclid and Allandale Avenues in East Cleveland. The original church still exists as a parlor for the newer Gothic Revival church. The southern end of the original cemetery is still occupied by the school and parish hall. The balance of these grounds was paved over and now rests beneath a parking lot at the rear of the building.

9

DEMALINE CEMETERY

SHELDEN/MCDOWELL/DIMLINE PLOT

Lat 41°32'47.774" N, long 81°24'48.945" W
41.546604, -81.413596
Status: Partially Accessible

The story behind the Demaline Cemetery is an interesting one, filled with contradictions and confusion. To begin with, the family name, as it appears on tombstones, was actually Dimline but has, over the years, changed to Dimaline and then to Demaline. All three variations of the name have been accepted. Furthermore, there were two other families that buried their dead on this site well before the Dimline family came to own this property. The first of these was the Shelden family.

Daniel Shelden was born in 1791 to Anthony and Mercy Phillips Shelden. At eighteen, he married Eliza Crouch, who sadly passed away six years later. His mother passed away the following year.

Daniel came to Mayfield Township in 1825 with his father; second wife, Elizabeth; and numerous children. They settled along the river, near the north end of the township. It was at the death of his second wife, on June 11, 1830, that this burial ground was established. The site selected was a hill beside the road that sat just to the north of his property; it was the highest point in the area. Daniel Shelden died five years after his second wife. At this, the Shelden property passed on to his son. The only other known Shelden burial on that plot is Daniel's father, Anthony, who passed away in 1848.

One of the earliest owners of the burial site was Frederick J. Willson, for whom the small community in the north end of Gates Mills was once named. Willson was born in 1807 in Phelps, Ontario County, New York, to George and Esther Willson. He traveled to Mayfield Township in 1830 with his younger sister, Harriet, and her husband, David McDowell. The year after their arrival, David built a store in the small community along the river, the first in Mayfield Township. Two years later, he and Frederick built a hotel, a gristmill and a sawmill along a millrace that they dug just to the south of the river bend, the ruins of which can still be seen today. Soon after, the small village became known as Macksville, in honor of its most enterprising resident, David McDowell.

In 1835, Frederick Willson sold the land that contained the cemetery to McDowell, who owned it for only the next eight years. McDowell sold the land, which comprised 135 acres, to Thomas Dimline on January 7, 1843. McDowell must have been ill at the time and wanted to put his affairs in order. He passed away just two months later, on March 16, 1843, at the age of thirty-seven. He left behind a widow and six children. He was the first person outside of the Shelden family to be buried in this lot. The name Macksville remained with the small village along the river until the 1860s, when it was changed to Willson's Mills.

In regard to the Dimline family, Thomas Dimline was born on January 27, 1788, in Thorne, Yorkshire, England, to William and Elizabeth Saul Dimline. In early 1808, he married Ann Pears, also of Yorkshire. Following the conclusion of the War of 1812, Thomas moved with his wife and children to the United States and ultimately settled in Mayfield, right around the time that he made his purchase from David McDowell.

The first burial in the graveyard from this family occurred on September 7, 1846, when Thomas and Ann's daughter Hannah passed away at thirty years of age. Recently, she had become the wife of John Walker of Mayfield. Her death was followed on Christmas Day by the death of her thirty-eight-year-old brother John. Thomas Dimline would only enjoy his property in Mayfield for five years after making his purchase. He died on August 28, 1848, and was likewise buried in the small hilltop cemetery. The next two Dimline family members to be buried there were two of Thomas and Ann's grandsons—Thomas, who died on January 12, 1851, and fifteen-year-old James, who died on September 8, 1856. These were the two eldest children of Thomas and Anna's son, William Dimline. On March 12, 1862, a neighbor named Olivia A. Van Avery, the twenty-seven-year-old wife of Oscar Almarion

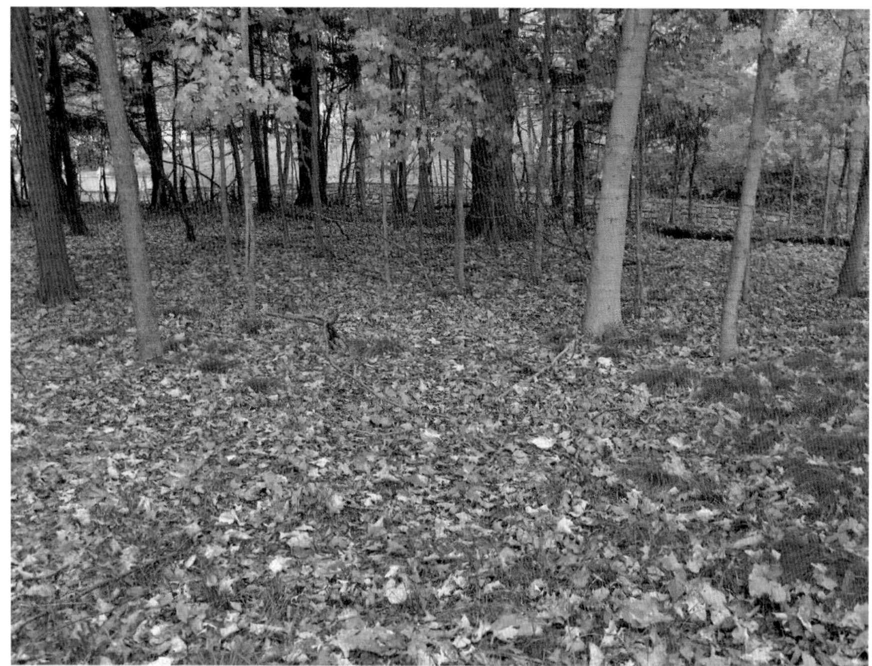

No trace remains at the original location of the Demaline Cemetery. *Author's collection.*

Van Avery, was buried there as well. Olivia's father was Diamon Wakeman, an area landowner, postmaster and justice of the peace. Ann Pears Dimline, Thomas's eighty-three-year-old widow, is the last person known to be buried at the Demaline Cemetery. She died in 1865.

In the years that followed, the land fell back into the hands of the Willson family and was eventually owned by Celia Waters. In June 1928, E.H. Sherman visited this site and documented what remained. According to the notes, all of the tombstones had fallen over. One was buried in the sod and illegible while another, the one for Ann Pears Dimline, was broken and buried too deep to be moved. Mrs. Homer Sullivan commented on this property in later years, stating that, in the 1950s, the cemetery property belonged to Phil Bruch (Edward Phillip Bruch Jr., a local aviation enthusiast). She stated that no stones were standing in 1928 and that the remaining stones had been taken to Gates Mills North Cemetery by 1971. The stones that could be located now stand in a chained-off area at the back of Gates Mills North Cemetery. Not located were the stones for the Shelden family or David McDowell. A memorial plaque has been placed there to honor these early pioneers.

Today, the site of the old Demaline Cemetery is only a nondescript hill on the west side of Chagrin River Road about six hundred feet south of Brigham Road in Gates Mills. At some point in its history, Chagrin River Road might have been widened, and a significant section of this burial ground might have been destroyed. This part of the cemetery, being on the western verge of the road, is accessible to the public. The balance of the graveyard, which rests on the hill, is private property and strictly off limits. Neither of these areas, on public or private property, gives any hint that this site was ever used as a cemetery.

10
BATTLES CEMETERY

BATTLES/RUSSELL BURYING GROUNDS

Lat 41°33'20.138" N, long 81°24'08.935" W
41.555594, -81.402482
Status: Strictly Off Limits!

Jedediah Russell, a native of New Hampshire, came to Mayfield Village in 1831 with his wife, Abigail Whiting, and son Caleb B. Russell's family. There they occupied a piece of land in the northeast corner of the township, owned by Samuel and Eunice Cole, where Caleb operated a cooperage and farmed the land. Shortly after settling, Abigail Whiting Russell passed away and was buried on a small, wooded knoll on the property. On September 27, 1844, Caleb's son Charles R. Russell passed and was also interred on that hill. Following the death of Jedediah Russell in September 1863, Caleb Russell decided to sell his land to his neighbors, the Battles family, and move with his wife and children to Willoughby. Excluded from this sale was a small schoolhouse on the property. Included in the sale was the old Russell family graveyard.

Luther Battles Sr., was born on October 17, 1792, in Swanzey, Cheshire County, New Hampshire, to Deland Battles and Sarah Grimes. When Luther was just seventeen years of age, his father passed away, and he moved with his widowed mother and sisters to Herkimer County, New York. In 1813, he enlisted to defend the border against the British at Sackett's Harbor. Four years later, he was married to Arethusa Porter and soon began a very large family.

Originally bound for Trumbull County, he found the land swampy and not to his liking. At this, he changed his plans and continued farther west, arriving in Mayfield Village in June 1834 with his wife, mother and eight children. Two more children would be born in the following years.

The small cemetery already on their land was added to on September 4, 1856, with the death of Luther's eighty-three-year-old mother, Sarah, who had since become the wife of Luther Woodworth of Euclid. Two months later, there was another interment, Luther's thirty-three-year-old daughter, Sarah, who was the wife of John Presley Jr.

After Luther Battles had purchased the farm in 1866, the adjoining cemetery primarily became the burial ground for the Battles family. The exceptions to this were neighbors Evan and Mary Jones and forty-one-year-old Daniel Turner, the second husband of Luther's daughter-in-law, who died on July 12, 1871. In all, thirteen members of the Battles family were laid to rest in this little cemetery. The last was Luther's eldest son, Edwin Deland Battles, who died on March 17, 1911, at the age of ninety.

That same year, the first removal from this cemetery took place with the exhumation of the remains of Luther Battles's son Newton, who had died during the first year of the Civil War. Newton's wife, Mary Stewart Battles, had passed away just six days before Edwin and was buried in Chesterland, where most of the family was now residing. Newton Battles was away at war when his son, Newton Jr., was born. Sadly, Newton Sr. died from fever at Camp Wickliffe, Kentucky, just four months after the birth of his son. Never having seen his father, Newton Battles Jr. ordered his father's casket to be opened when it was exhumed and was astonished to discover that, after fifty years of being in the ground, the remains were perfectly preserved. Also relocated at this time were the remains of Newton and Mary's six-year-old daughter, Lydia Mallisa, who had died in January 1860.

In 1959, most of what could be located at the Battles Cemetery was relocated to the Chester Township Cemetery in Chesterland and was reinterred in section A, lots 269 and 270. A number of fragmented headstones were left behind, as were the footstones for Evan and Mary Jones. Some of these stone fragments ended up in the barn of Mr. Jewett, who owned the adjacent land during the mid-twentieth century.

This cemetery is actually composed of two separate burial grounds. There is, of course, the one that the Russell family had sold to Luther Battles, but there is also a second one, which Luther Battles Jr. and his wife, Catherine, sold to Luther Battles Sr., Rufus Mapes and Evan Jones in 1877. While Luther

Battles Sr. and Evan Jones were ultimately buried here with their families, it is uncertain why Rufus Mapes's name appears on this title transfer. To begin with, Mapes had passed away three years earlier, and even then, he had been buried on his own farm, which was on the other side of the township. The

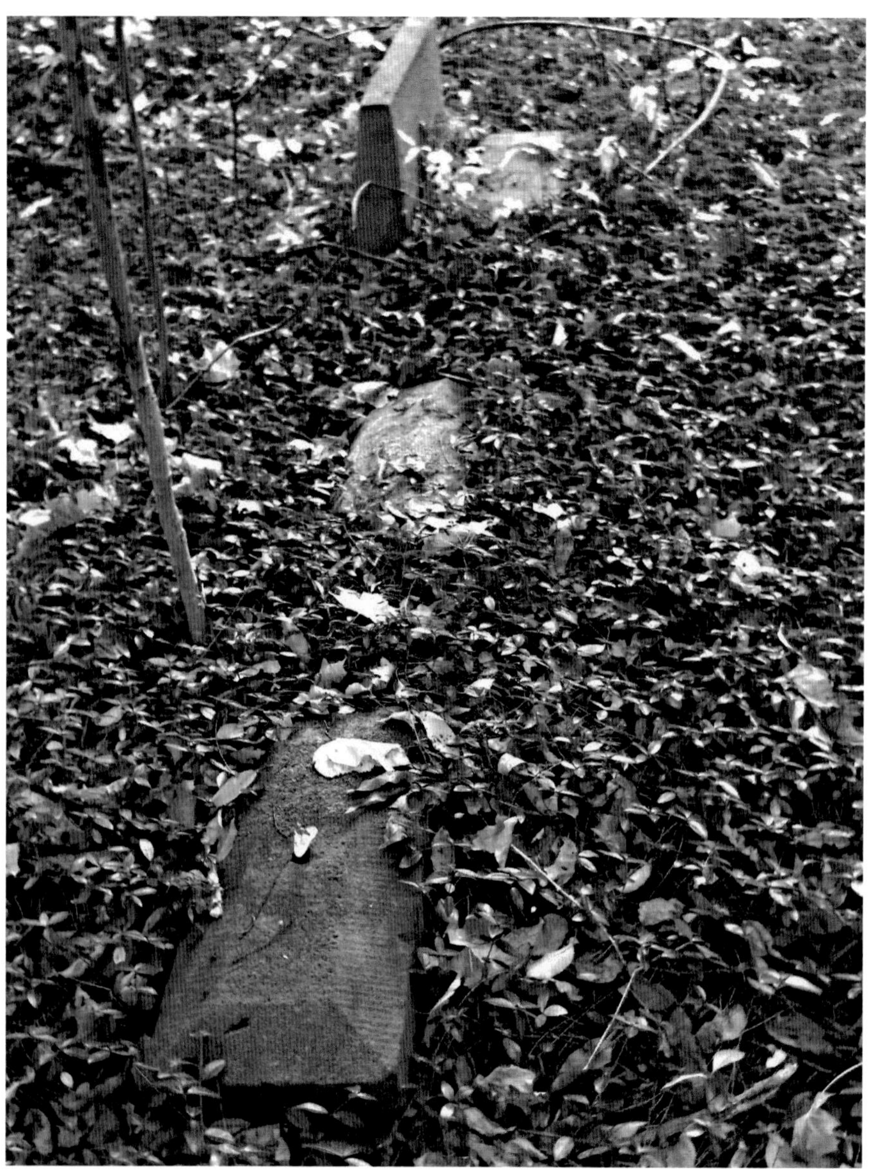

Hidden among the myrtle lie the remains of many tombstones at the Battles Cemetery. *Author's collection.*

only supposition is that it had something to do with Luther's wife, Catherine, being Rufus's daughter. Perhaps it was intended that this was to become the future burial site of the Mapes descendants as well. As it was, Rufus Mapes didn't repose on his own land for very long. His grave would eventually be moved to the Mayfield Union Cemetery.

Over the ensuing years, the reservation of these two lots continued to show up on title transfers but was eventually omitted altogether, appearing for the last time in 1924, when Murl Rogers transferred the property to James W. Rogers. A search on property lines still shows these two lots as being separate and in the possession of the Battles family. The first of these, the original Russell lot, is about one-sixth of an acre, while the second is composed of just over 2,500 square feet.

Today, the Battles Cemetery exists on a wooded hillock with creeping myrtle covering the forest floor, near the north end of Battles Road in Gates Mills. Scattered around the south end of the grounds are the bases of many of the headstones that were moved to Chesterland. Here and there, broken pieces of limestone markers can be found, testaments to what this land once was. Still standing along the very southern verge of the hill, almost completely hidden from view, are two broken and worn sandstone grave markers, the names they bore have long since faded.

Resting at the far north end of the grounds is a broken urn and a damaged limestone pedestal that once held a large monument. This section was the original Russell family cemetery. No gravestones exist here anymore; they might have been moved to the S.O.M. Road Cemetery in Willoughby Hills where the rest of the Russell family is now buried.

Although the actual cemetery is still, legally, in the possession of the Battles family, the surrounding properties are in private hands and are occupied by residences. While there was once an access road to and from this burial ground, it has since been taken over by the property that adjoins it on the west side of Battles Road. This access road is now the driveway for that property. In short, the cemetery is no longer accessible to the public without running a high risk of being arrested for trespassing. The area is patrolled regularly, roadside parking is prohibited in Gates Mills, and therefore, readers are strongly advised not to visit this site.

Of the eighteen people who were interred at the Battles Cemetery, seven were not relocated to Chesterland. Those not moved were the two members of the Russell family; Sarah Presley; Daniel Turner; Edwin Battles's second wife, Chloe; and two of Luther's grandsons, eight-year-old Ralph Tinker and ten-year-old Franklin Battles. If Franklin Battles is in fact still buried at the Battles Cemetery, then perhaps the epitaph on his now-lost headstone was correct in its words:

A dutiful son, a child most dear
Young in life, he's buried here
Earth holds his ashes here in trust
Until Christ shall gather up his dust.

11

EUCLID STOP 8 CEMETERY

FIRST BAPTIST CHURCH AND SOCIETY BURYING GROUND

Lat 41°34'18.674" N, long 81°32'14.968" W
41.571854, -81.537491
Status: Accessible with Caution

The name "Stop 8 Cemetery" is inaccurate. The name is derived from the concept that it was located some distance west of Chardon Road, which was Stop 10 on the Cleveland, Painesville and Eastern Interurban Railroad. While it is true that it was west of the road, it wasn't far enough west to be even close to Stop 8. In fact, it was located only about three hundred feet to the west. While it was in existence, it was never referred to by its railroad stop designation; the true name was the First Baptist Church and Society Burying Ground.

This small graveyard was first established on John Wilcox's farm. This occurred on April 4, 1811, with the death and burial of a forty-three-year-old woman named Rhoda Kittredge, wife of Amaziah Porter. Amaziah followed her to the grave in 1837.

The second burial occurred on August 19, 1821, with the death of thirty-four-year-old Elizabeth Pelton, Wilcox's first wife. Her death was followed on October 3 of that year by the passing of two-year-old Clinton Treat, the son of John Wilcox's neighbors, William and Lucy Treat. Sadly, Lucy passed away just twelve days later, becoming the fourth person interred there. On February 20, 1822, Rebecca Coleman Sage, wife of John Sage, passed and was buried there.

A few months later, John Wilcox sold the land to the First Baptist Church and Society of Euclid for the grand sum of six cents. That July, William Treat found a new bride in John Wilcox's late wife's sister, Sally Pelton. There were three men placed on the building committee for the new church: John Wilcox, William Treat and their brother-in-law, Seth Doane Pelton.

Three more of William Treat's children were interred in this cemetery over the course of the next twenty years: Sanford Treat (1821–31), Clarissa Treat (born and died in 1832) and Fridena Treat (1826–41.) William's wife, Sally, followed these children on August 29, 1854. The following year, Sally and William's eldest son, Charles Clinton Treat, died while living in Vermont. Though he was buried in that state, a tombstone was placed in the Baptist burying ground as a memorial to his life. William Treat ultimately moved to Topeka, Kansas, and died there in October 1873. His grave in Topeka Cemetery is marked with a federal headstone that gives his service record from the War of 1812.

Someone of notoriety buried in the Baptist Cemetery was Revolutionary War veteran Jacob Coleman. Private Coleman enlisted on September 15, 1780, in Hackensack, New Jersey, where he served for three years under Colonel "Light Horse Harry" Lee. He and his wife, Deborah Herron, arrived in Euclid about 1810. Deborah died there in 1821. Jacob Coleman passed away in June 1835, and both were interred in the cemetery. Many of their descendants were likewise interred in the burial ground. Another notable buried there was Seth Doane Pelton, who had served on the building committee for the Baptist church. Many of his descendants also repose on the site. Original landowner John Wilcox passed away on February 20, 1869, and was buried there.

Following the opening of the Euclid Cemetery in 1864, there was a movement throughout the township to have graves relocated to one central burial ground. Those who owned lots in the Baptist cemetery now purchased three lots in the Euclid Cemetery (C15 to C17) on March 16, 1876, and began to remove their loved ones to that site. This primarily included members of the Coleman, Pelton and Sumner families.

In 1881, the old Baptist burial ground entered a state of controversy when the New York, Chicago and St. Louis Railroad was sent through the area and crossed the northwestern grounds of the cemetery. At this, the graves of the Wilcoxes and Jacob Coleman were relocated to Euclid Cemetery. Unfortunately, Jacob's wife Deborah's grave was not located and remained at the cemetery. She now likely rests beneath the railroad tracks. The last known burial to have taken place here occurred in 1888 with the death of Mary Porter Pelton, wife of the late Seth Doane Pelton.

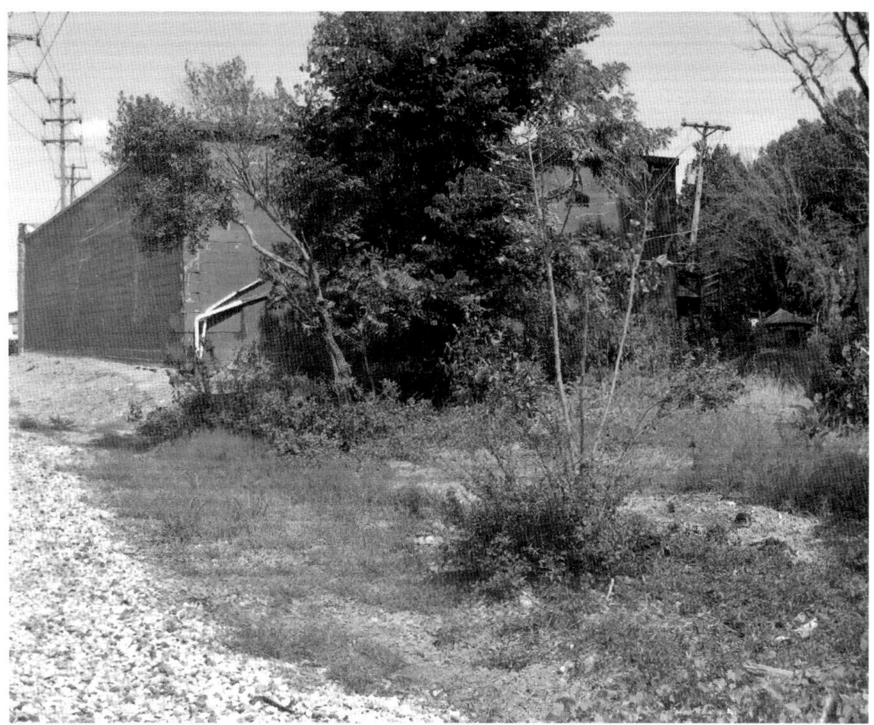

The site of the First Baptist Church and Society Burying Ground of Euclid now exists as a weed-choked lot behind a building on Chardon Road. *Author's collection.*

In the years that followed, the old Baptist burying ground fell victim to vandalism and was used as a playground for local children. Then, on June 21, 1926, the Baptist church sold the land containing the cemetery to the Teachout Realty and Investment Company, which promptly sold it to the Duplex Manufacturing Foundry Company.

In 1934, a survey was made of the site, and a few tombstones from the old burial ground still remained. These belonged to Rhoda Kittredge Porter and Sally Pelton Treat. Also remaining was the stone for Charles Clinton Treat and two others that were barely legible. One simply said "age 26 yrs," possibly Abner Nieuman Sumner (1834–55), and the other bore the name "Madison." Since then, Rhoda Porter and Sally Treat have been relocated to Euclid Cemetery. Sadly, the graves of William Treat's first wife, Lucy; his three children; and Amaziah Porter were not located and therefore likely remain on the site.

Today, the First Baptist Church and Society Burying Ground exists as a small wedge of land at the rear of 1410 Chardon Road in Euclid. The site is bounded on the northwest by the Norfolk Southern Railroad and on the south by the running track and football field of Central Middle School. A small, triangular building now occupies the northeast corner of the site. The ground is very uneven, and trains pass with high frequency. No trace of this cemetery remains.

12
PETERS FARM CEMETERY

OLD PELTON'S CORNERS BURIAL GROUND

Lat 41°34'31.966" N, long 81°29'50.658" W
41.575546, -81.497405
Status: Accessible with Caution

Another of the many cemeteries located throughout old Euclid Township is the Peters Farm Cemetery. This small burial ground was said to be located near the intersection of Chardon and Richmond Roads. The earliest recognized burial that took place there occurred in 1817 with the interment of a member of the Gray family. The only Gray family in the township at that time was that of Thomas Gray.

Thomas Jefferson Gray had come to Euclid in the first years of its existence, and it was there, on May 28, 1809, that he married Cassina Elizabeth Dille, daughter of David Dille and Nancy Viers. Thomas Gray was the son of John Gray, who was famed for being the last surviving veteran of the American Revolution. The Gray family headstone was still identifiable in the early 1900s, but all that could be made out was the last name and the date referred to above. Most likely, this stone marked the burial site of one of Thomas and Cassina's children. The Grays did not remain in Euclid Township but relocated to Harrison County, Ohio, shortly after this burial occurred.

It should be noted that, while members of the Gray family were buried there, they did not own the land. The first person to own the property was Abraham Bishop. Bishop had come to Euclid Township in 1809 and, the following year, erected a sawmill along the creek, just south of Chardon

Road. Abraham Bishop owned the land for only five years. His nineteen-year-old son John sold it to the newly arrived deacon, Jonathan Pelton.

Jonathan Pelton was born on June 10, 1759, in Chatham, Middlesex County, Connecticut, to Joseph and Hannah Penfield Pelton. On December 4, 1782, he married Elizabeth Doane. They had no fewer than twelve children. One of these children, Seth Doane Pelton, had come to Euclid a few years earlier with his wife, Mary Porter, and farmed the area that his parents would soon occupy. Seth Pelton, as previously stated, had been one of the founders of the First Baptist Church and Society of Euclid. After Deacon Jonathan Pelton purchased all 250 acres of the Bishop farm, that whole section of the township became known as Pelton's Corners.

The first Pelton to be buried in this cemetery was Jonathan and Elizabeth's daughter Mercy Parker Pelton, who died on October 20, 1820, just five days shy of her nineteenth birthday. Deacon Pelton passed away in September 1830 and was likewise buried there. His wife joined him ten years later.

In all, there were seven members of the Pelton family interred in the lot, including the Coopers, Jonathan and Elizabeth's daughter Beulah's family. It was also the likely burial site of nine members of the neighboring Stephen White family who died between 1826 and 1865.

Following the death of Deacon Jonathan Pelton, the land passed into the hands of his son, Seth Doane Pelton. It remained so until June 20, 1866, when he sold off the area that contained the small cemetery. The little burial plot consisted of $^{43}/_{100}$ of an acre with a right of way to and from the cemetery on Chardon Road leading from Euclid Village to Chardon. The new owners were Nathaniel and Eliza Merrills.

Two later burials were those of seventy-five-year-old Leffie Witheral Stray, wife of James Stray, and her three-year-old grandson, Nelson F. Stray. Leffie's death occurred on July 4, 1865, and Nelson's occurred in August 1871. When James Stray died in 1873, a lot was purchased at Euclid Cemetery (C52), and he was interred there. Both James and Leffie Stray's names appear on one tombstone at that cemetery, but when a survey was done of the old burial ground in 1928, her headstone was still present. It was made of beautiful marble and lay in a pool of water. Another large stone, about six or seven inches thick, was lying facedown and was too heavy to be moved without a lever. This is possibly the one for the Gray family burial.

It might seem strange that Leffie Witheral Stray has a tombstone and an epitaph in two separate cemeteries, but it really isn't all that odd. Either her remains were relocated to rest beside those of her husband's at Euclid

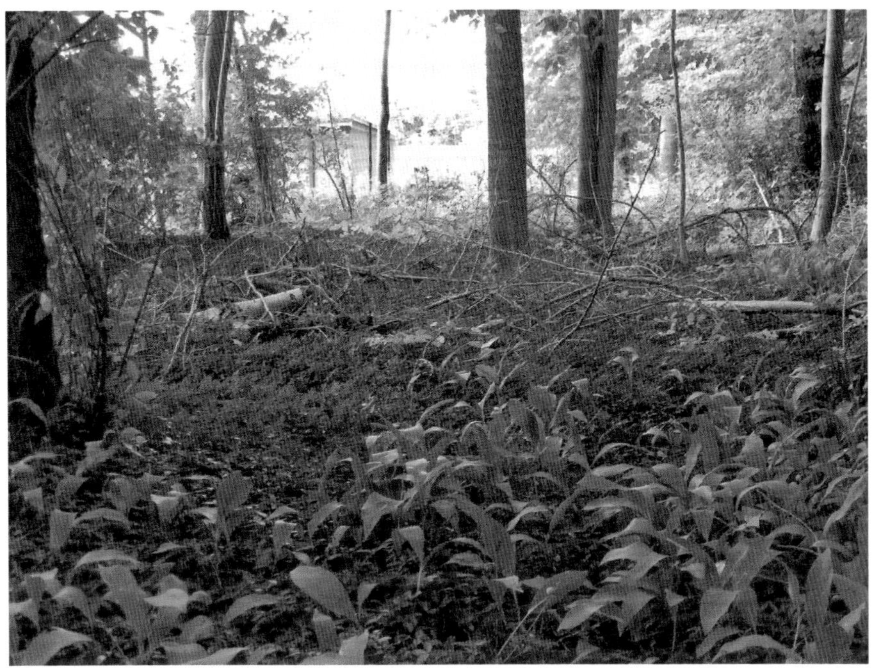

Creeping myrtle covers the site of the Peters Farm Cemetery. *Author's collection.*

Cemetery and the original tombstone was simply left behind, or she was never moved and the epitaph on her husband's gravestone was placed there for informational purposes only. It should be noted that the Gray headstone was never moved to Euclid Cemetery.

The Merrill family owned the land until 1876, when they sold it to Wenzel Klipec, who possessed the property for four years before selling it to Jacob and Barbara Peters in 1880. From then on, the area was locally known as the Peters Farm, thus the name of the cemetery. Jacob Peters, who passed away on March 30, 1894, was the last person known to be buried there. How long he rested on the site is unknown; his family purchased a lot at Euclid Cemetery (D102) shortly after his death. He now rests there beside his wife and children. Most of the Peltons, Coopers and Whites were likewise relocated to Euclid Cemetery, but there's no telling who or what was left behind.

Many years later, the farmhouse, barn and outbuildings were demolished, and Richmond Road was extended northwest through the middle of the farm. Off to the side of this new road sat what remained of the old cemetery. Ruins were still visible through the 1940s. In the 1960s,

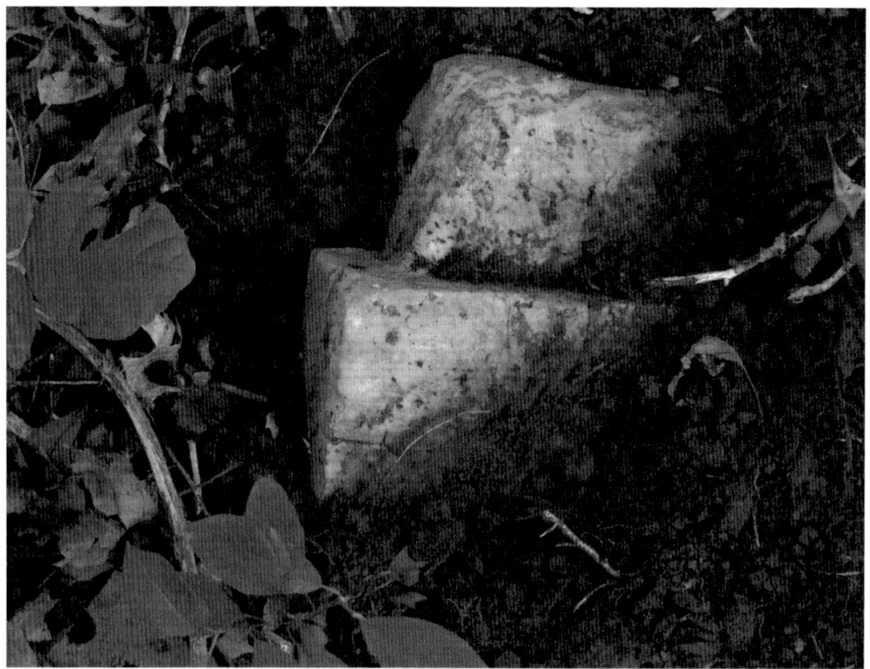

Small traces of the Peters Farm Cemetery can still be seen today. *Author's collection.*

a Lawson's convenience store was eventually built on the front of the site at 218 Richmond Road. It is believed that any tombstones that could be located were taken away and used elsewhere for walkways.

Today, the old Peters Farm is no longer in Euclid but is now a part of Richmond Heights. The former cemetery site rests in a patch of woods just behind a daycare center (218 Richmond Road) and a gas station located just to the south. The area is covered in creeping myrtle. The ground is uneven, and there are many tripping hazards. One should exercise caution when visiting this site.

13
RICHMOND CEMETERY

A VILLAGE NAMESAKE

Lat 41°33'14.249" N, long 81°29'49.942" W
41.553958, -81.497206
Status: Fully Accessible

Elihu Richmond was born in Taunton, Bristol County, Massachusetts, on June 22, 1770, to Edmund Richmond and Abigail Wood. His father was a lieutenant during the American Revolution and had served his country between 1776 and 1780. His mother, on the other hand, was a descendant of *Mayflower* passengers John Alden and Priscilla Mullins. Elihu married Betsey Robbins in Partridgefield, Massachusetts, on April 10, 1794. They soon began raising a family.

On July 9, 1812, Elihu purchased 316 acres in Euclid Township from the State of Connecticut and began to make plans for the future. He, his wife and six children set out from Peru, Berkshire County, Massachusetts, in late 1814 and arrived in January of the following year. That first winter must have been rough, but through all of the trials that faced settlers on the frontier, the Richmond family managed to build a log cabin and pull through the hard season. This log cabin, though greatly modified over the years, still stands today at 25625 Highland Road in present-day Richmond Heights.

For ten years, the Richmond family continued to grow and thrive in their new home. It wasn't until 1825 that the family experienced great loss. This occurred with the death of two-year-old Cynthia Shepherd, a daughter of Elihu and Betsey's daughter Matilda. At once, a small burial site was selected

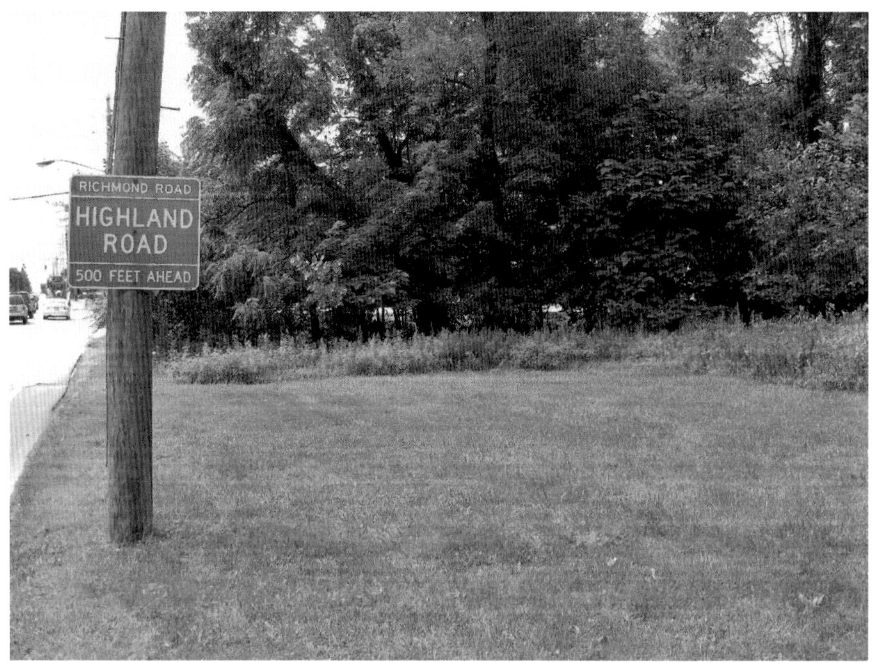

This grassy lot along Richmond Road was once the site of the Richmond Cemetery. *Author's collection.*

along a north and southbound road on the eastern verge of their property, just to the north of what would one day be known as Claribel Creek. The next interment in this cemetery didn't take place for another twelve years. It occurred with the passing of four-year-old Martha Weston, a daughter of Elihu and Betsey's daughter Sally, in 1837.

On May 7, 1838, Elihu Richmond died. Two deaths occurred within months of each other in 1842—Elihu and Betsey's son Seth died on April 22, and six-year-old Mary Weston, Martha's sister, died on August 4. Elihu and Betsey's son Levi died on January 5, 1844, just three months shy of his fortieth birthday. In 1846, Caroline Shepherd, Cynthia's eighteen-year-old sister, was added to the ever-growing family plot.

Olive Sprague, the first wife of Elihu and Betsey's son Edmund, passed away on April 11, 1848, less than one month before her forty-third birthday. In 1851, forty-seven-year-old William Robertson died and was likewise interred there. Robertson was born in England in 1804 and had simply been a neighbor and friend of the Richmond family. He is likely the only person buried there that was not a family relation.

It should also be noted that Elihu Richmond had once had an older brother named Abner, who remained in Massachusetts and died there. Following his death in 1840, Abner's widow, Rachel Ferguson Richmond, made the journey to Ohio with her children and settled very near to her late husband's family. Both Rachel and her infant granddaughter, Jeanette F. Richmond, passed away in 1852 and were interred in the Richmond Cemetery. Joining them on June 9, 1856, was Susan, Jeanette's seventeen-year-old sister. Just two

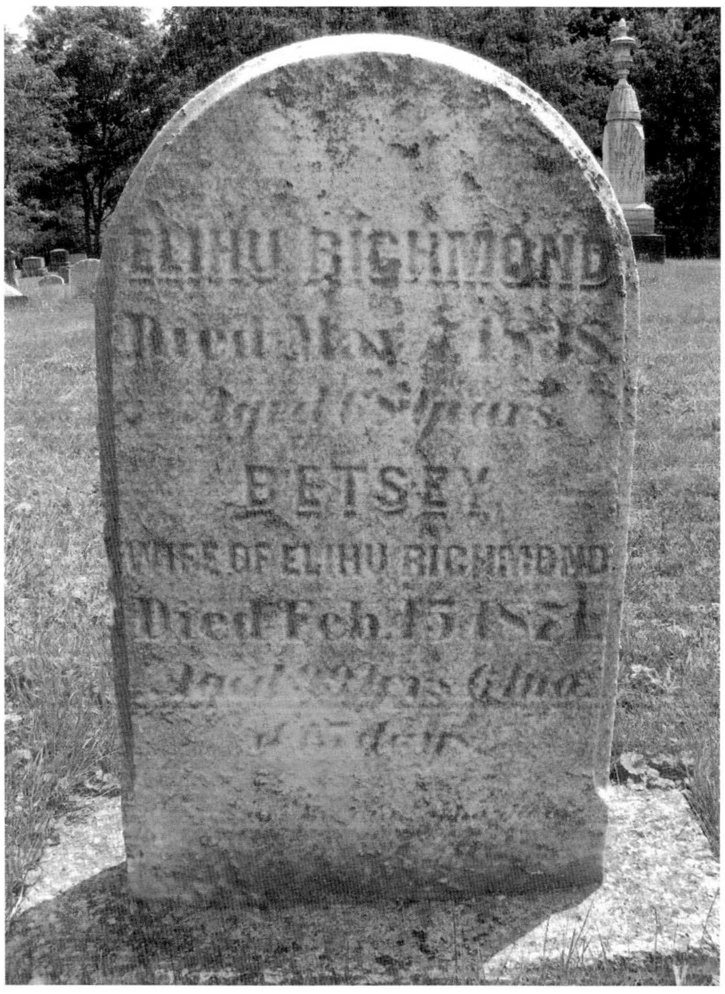

The headstone of Elihu and Betsey Richmond now stands above their grave site in Euclid Cemetery. *Author's collection.*

weeks earlier, the family had experienced a loss with the death of Charles A. Weston, the eldest son of Elihu and Betsey's daughter Sally.

It was another three years before anyone else was buried at the Richmond Cemetery. That next interment occurred with the death of five-year-old Francis A. Richmond on October 8, 1859. Francis was a granddaughter of Elihu and Betsey's son Edmund. Sadly, Edmund Richmond also lost two sons between 1862 and 1863. The first to die was Warren F. Richmond, who was killed at the Battle of Cedar Mountain, Virginia, on August 9, 1862. His brother Orlando died the following June.

The last known burial there was that of nine-and-a-half-month-old Willie Orlando Pelton, on February 20, 1864. Named after his late uncle, young Willie was the son of Orlando's sister Eliza and her husband, George Pelton. Shortly after this burial, four lots were purchased at the newly opened Euclid Cemetery (lots A11, A12, A22 and A23.) All further deaths in the family were interred there.

It is likely that the burials from this old cemetery were relocated to Euclid Cemetery sometime in the early 1870s following the deaths of Edmund Richmond's second wife, Elvira Everett, and his mother, Betsey Robbins Richmond, who died in 1871, less than six months shy of becoming a centenarian. The four lots at Euclid Cemetery now contain the remains of all who were once buried at the old Richmond Cemetery—with the exceptions of Seth Richmond and Cynthia and Caroline Shepherd. It is presumed that their graves could not be located and still remain on the site. Of further note: while there is an epitaph for Warren F. Richmond at Euclid Cemetery, his remains were never recovered from Cedar Mountain, Virginia, and there is an empty grave in section A11 where it was hoped that he would one day be interred.

The original Richmond Cemetery site now exists as a small, grassy field on the west side of Richmond Road near Highland Road. This field sits just north of the Richmond Heights Post Office and Claribel Creek, which runs to the north of the post office entrance.

14

CROSIER CEMETERY

A NEW ENGLAND PATRIOT'S BURIAL SITE

Lat 41°58'00.451" N, long 81°32'12.649" W
41.966792, -81.536847
Status: Accessible with Caution

John M. Crosier was born on October 23, 1750, in the village of Dorchester, near Boston, Massachusetts. It was here that he had worked in his earliest years as a blacksmith. Business opportunities eventually carried him to the village of Dedham, where, on April 13, 1775, he wed Fanny Whiting. Just five nights later, an alarm was raised from the street outside of his home. This messenger carried but one phrase: "The British are coming!" It was not Paul Revere who had delivered this warning, as he had been riding in the north to Lexington and Concord, but another rider who had received the message from Abel Prescott Jr. at Farmingham. Upon hearing the alert, twenty-four-year-old John bid farewell to his new bride, took up his musket and made haste for Lexington Green, where he arrived the following morning just in time to meet the British. The young private was among those brave men in the Continental Line who fired the first shots in a war that would form a nation.

Following his participation that June at the Battle of Bunker Hill, John Crosier was promoted to the rank of ensign. He soon rose to the rank of second lieutenant and was placed in Crane's Regiment of Artillery. He had spent the terrible winter of 1777–78 with General George Washington at Valley Forge and was present at Yorktown in 1781. At the Battles of Germantown and Monmouth, he had served as acting captain.

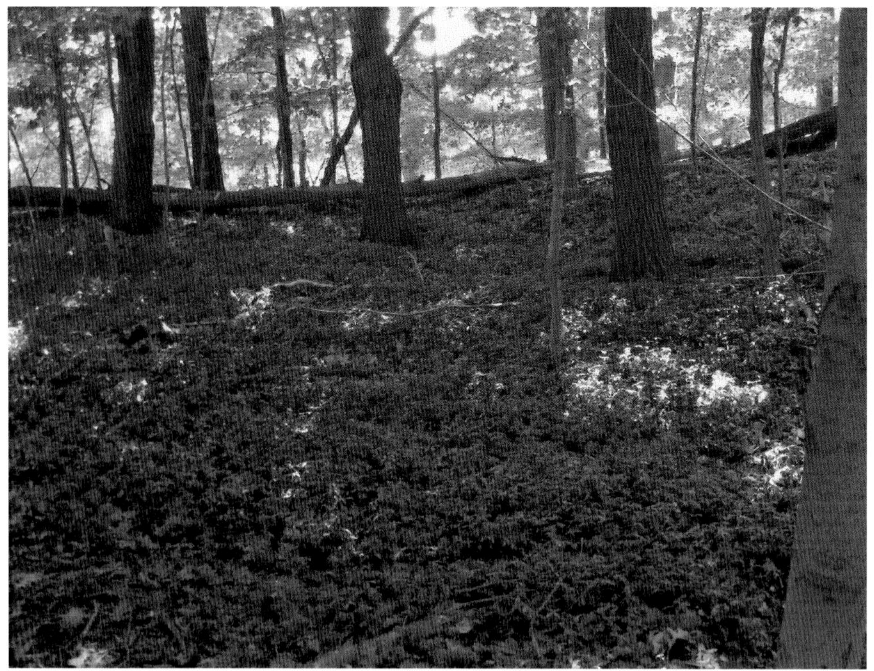

It was from this commanding view that Lieutenant John Crosier once took his repose. *Author's collection.*

At the close of the war, he returned to his wife in Dedham, Massachusetts, and continued expanding his family. He and Fanny had ten children before her passing in 1806 at the age of fifty-three. Two years after her death, he married Druscilla Gleason, who died two and a half years after their union. His third wife was thirty-seven-year-old Sarah Groves Bemis. The two wed on June 25, 1811, in Chester, Massachusetts. Five years later, John set out for Ohio, where he settled in Euclid with his wife, thirty-four-year-old son Jason Crosier and Jason's family.

Lieutenant Crosier and his third wife, Sarah, both passed away in 1823, leaving behind three small children. They were buried in a small lot on Jason Crosier's land. At least two other burials are known to have taken place here: Sarah Jane Crosier, John's twenty-four-year-old great granddaughter, who died in 1857, and Martha Easton Crosier, the first wife of John's grandson, Henry, who died in 1860 at the age of thirty-four.

When Euclid Cemetery was opened, Sarah Jane Crosier's parents relocated her remains in the new family plot (A5). Mayor Wilson Elmer Crosier, a fifth-generation descendant of Lieutenant John M. Crosier, had the graves that could be located in the old Crosier Cemetery exhumed and transferred to Euclid Cemetery in 1908. These included Lieutenant John and Martha Easton Crosier. They were reinterred in lot D4. A government-issued headstone that notes his military service now marks Lieutenant Crosier's grave. The remains of John Crosier's third wife, Sarah Groves Bemis Crosier, were not moved to this cemetery. They likely still remain on the original site. The only mention of the small family cemetery in any archival document appears in a title transfer from 1858, which describes a piece of land bordering Paul Crosier's property at the north corner of "the cemetery."

Today, the old Crosier Cemetery exists as a small wooded lot on the east side of old Glen Ridge Road, between Euclid Cemetery and Highland Road. Walking east into the woods from old Glen Ridge Road directly parallel with the drive that bisects Euclid Cemetery, one first discovers the ruins of an old house. This was the Hay family home. Continuing northeast from the foundation of the Hay house, the ground begins to decline and ends at a high promontory overlooking Highland Road. This is the exact site of the Crosier Cemetery. The ground is covered in creeping myrtle and is fairly uneven, and the woods are quite dense. It was from this commanding view that a New England Patriot once took his repose.

15

SPRING FAMILY CEMETERY

THE GRAVES IN THE GARDEN

Lat 41°32'00.344" N, long 81°30'59.471" W
41.553420, -81.516520
Status: Fully Accessible

When Alfred and Rose Mosbacher purchased the house at 25309 Highland Road in Richmond Heights back in 1913, they must have thought it was a quiet location with nothing out of the ordinary. That thought couldn't have been further from the truth. Within days, neighbors were coming up to the house and introducing themselves. In passing, several mentioned that there had once been a cemetery where their garden was now located. This shocked the Mosbachers. The last owner, John Bartlett, had said nothing of this to them. Eventually, a search was done in their garden, but no tombstones could be found and for a very good reason.

To begin this story, we need to go back to January 8, 1799. On this day, Virgil Nigel Spring was born in Peru, Berkshire County, Massachusetts, to Sylvester Omar Spring Sr. and Sarah Dibble. He would eventually find his way to Euclid Township. On November 11, 1825, he wed Mary Richmond, the daughter of his father's friend, Elihu Richmond. Six children were born to this union.

Following their wedding, the Springs settled on land that was owned by Mary's brother Edmund. Soon after, Virgil Spring and his brother-in-law Edmund Richmond built a mill on the creek that crossed the property.

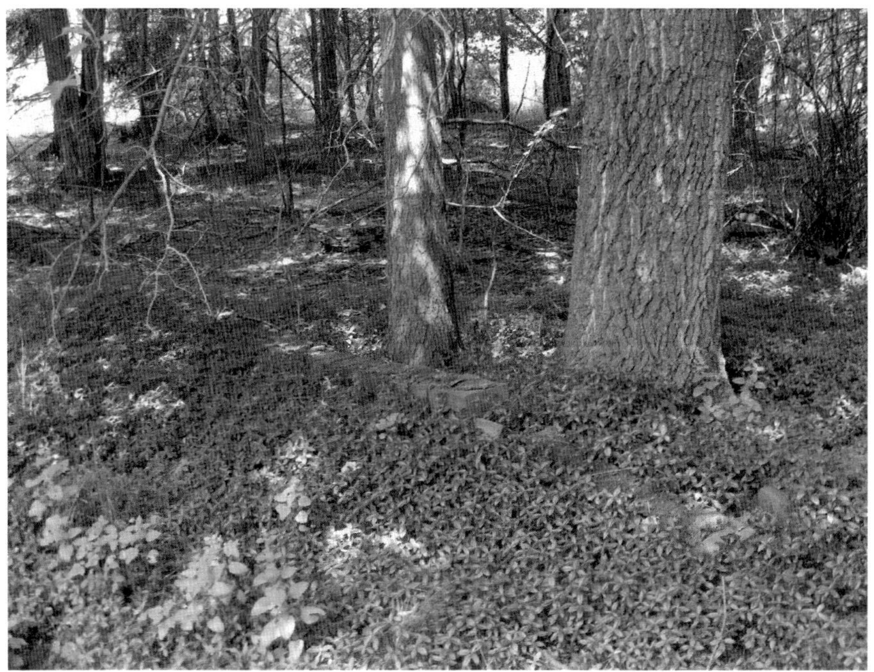

The site of the Spring Family Cemetery. *Author's collection.*

In 1841, Virgil's parents, Sylvester and Sarah, arrived from Massachusetts. Having no descendants living near them, they thought it best to sell their home and join their son and his family in Euclid. Six years later, Virgil Spring purchased the lands he'd been occupying from his brother-in-law and now owned the farm and mill outright.

On April 17, 1850, a small family cemetery was established on the property with the death of Virgil's mother, Sarah Dibble Spring. On February 2, 1854, twenty-three-year-old Albert Spring, a son of Virgil and Mary, followed her to the grave. The third person to be buried in the Spring Family Cemetery was not a family member at all. Her name was Francis Levesque, a friend and neighbor; she died in 1859 at the age of sixty-four. The final interment was that of Virgil's father, Sylvester Omar Spring Sr. His death occurred on September 15, 1861.

In July 1864, Virgil Nigel Spring sold his farm in Euclid Township to Frank Verbsky and moved to East Cleveland. That December, he purchased a family lot (A10) in Euclid Cemetery and had the remains that were originally buried on his property exhumed and reinterred in the new lot. The tall limestone Spring family marker now stands on that cemetery lot; thus, no stones remained in the Mosbachers' garden.

In 2013, the Friends of Euclid Creek purchased the property at 25309 Highland Road, and the house was demolished soon after. The eight-acre property now exists as the Redstone Run Highland Reserve.

16

SILAS JOHNSON FAMILY CEMETERY

MAYFIELD ROAD

Lat 41°31'11.797" N, long 81°29'26.556" W
41.519944, -81.490710
Status: Fully Accessible

On a June day in 1927, steam shovel operators working on Mayfield Road in South Euclid made a startling discovery. While cutting into the low embankment on the side of the road at Stop 13, one of the steam shovels unearthed a pair of coffins. Immediately, the machinery was backed away, and crews continued to carefully uncover what had been found.

The first coffin contained a human skull and about a dozen bones. The other had collapsed, and nothing recognizable could be seen. The exact amount of excavating done on the site is unknown, but these were the only graves discovered that day, and no tombstones could be located.

South Euclid marshal August Weigner acknowledged that the site had been a cemetery between seventy-five and one hundred years earlier. This puts the property in the hands of Silas Johnson, who possessed the land from 1836 to 1851. The previous owners, Joel and Rhoda Rush, resided in Geauga County and never lived on the land.

Silas Johnson had come to Ohio with his wife, Asenath Abel, and their children from New York State in 1831. The 1840 census shows him living on the land, in what was still Euclid Township, with his wife and four daughters. Ten years later, he still lived there but with only two daughters; his wife had passed away. It's likely that at least one of these coffins contained the remains of Asenath Abel Johnson.

Today, the site is currently the intersection of Mayfield Road and Henning Drive, just east of Richmond Road. Incidentally, the skull ended up becoming an ornament on the desk of the South Euclid marshal.

17

BLISS CEMETERY

MOVED AT A LATER DATE

Lat 41°34'17.659" N, long 81°31'40.166" W
41.571572, -81.527824
Status: Partially Accessible

There has been much debate about whether this cemetery actually existed, as the descendants of the Bliss family do not recall it. However, strong evidence exists that it did.

Aaron Sage Bliss was born on March 19, 1797, in Chatham, Connecticut. His father was Daniel Bliss, a Revolutionary War veteran who had enlisted three times during the struggle for independence. His mother, whose last name Sage is all that is known, died in 1800 while giving birth to Aaron's brother, Daniel. Aaron married Harriet Akins in 1817 and arrived in the small village of Euclid Creek around 1823.

The cemetery was established in 1826 after the death of Charles Sage Bliss, the four-year-old son of Aaron and Harriet. More than twenty years passed before any further burials occurred there—two of Aaron and Harriet's daughters, Frances Bliss Wilson and Esther Bliss Akins, who died in 1849 and 1850, respectively. Aaron Sage Bliss followed his children to the grave on September 2, 1853.

The farm, as well as the property that the cemetery occupied, was passed on to Aaron's son Henry Dwight Bliss. The graveyard received just two more burials before the family began interring their dead at the Euclid Cemetery. The first was Hanna Marie Farrind Bliss, the wife of

Aaron and Harriet's son George, who died in 1856. The other was Aaron and Harriet's daughter Harriet M. Bliss, who died in 1872. Harriet Akins Bliss, Aaron Sage Bliss's wife, died in North Ridgeville in 1871 and was buried there beside her son George, with whom she lived at the time of her passing.

Henry Dwight Bliss decided to divide his land and gave half of it to his son Eugene. When Henry died in 1892, his share of the property was willed to his wife, Anna.

Here's where the overwhelming evidence that points to the existence of this cemetery comes into play.

On November 11, 1903, Eugene sold a strip of land measuring 15 feet by 153 feet back to his mother. This strip of land ran between their properties. The title transfer was finally received by the Cuyahoga County Recorder's Office on April 16, 1904. Just three days later, the graves of Esther, Harriet M., Frances and Hanna were reinterred at the Euclid Cemetery in lot D9. Cemetery records do not indicate where these graves were relocated from, but the dates and the size of the property in question strongly point to them having come from this 15-foot-wide strip of land that ran between the two properties. It should be noted that Aaron Sage Bliss and his four-year-old son, Charles, were not reinterred in the Euclid Cemetery. Their graves cannot be located and are likely still on that site.

The original location of this little family burial ground now sits between two houses immediately to the east of the Corrigan-Deighton Funeral Home on Euclid Avenue. It exists as a slight, grassy rise beside the sidewalk and is crowned by a large maple tree. While it is on private property, a stroll along the sidewalk is all one needs to view the site.

18
KELLOGG FAMILY CEMETERY

HILLCREST UNITED METHODIST CHURCH

Lat 41°31'07.100" N, long 81°31'12.335" W
41.518639, -81.520093
Status: Fully Accessible

John Kellogg was born in Bethel, Fairfield County, Connecticut, in 1764 to Ezra and Ann Judd Kellogg. For a few years of his adult life, he lived in Lafayette, New York, before coming to Euclid Township in 1830 with his second wife, Esther Pixley. His first wife, Elizabeth Pickett, had died in New York just a few years earlier. The following year, John's thirty-six-year-old son Ezra arrived from New York with his wife and children and purchased the farm next to John and Esther.

In 1840, John sold his farm to his son; he passed away in March 1843. Four years later, Ezra's wife, Catherine McKown, passed away at the age of fifty-two. Both were interred in a small cemetery on the Kellogg farm. Other burials known to have taken place there are Ezra Kellogg; Maria Kellogg Ingram, Ezra and Catherine's daughter; and Maria's first husband, John Wesley Corbett, who died in the 1850s. It is also likely that Esther Pixley Kellogg is buried there, but no death record for her was located.

In 1874, the Kellogg family sold their farm to M.A. Hart. Excluded from this sale was the half acre of land that was being used as the cemetery. The little burial ground stayed in the family until November 1898, when it was sold to the trustees of the Methodist Episcopal Church of South Euclid to build a new church. One stipulation in this agreement was that the church

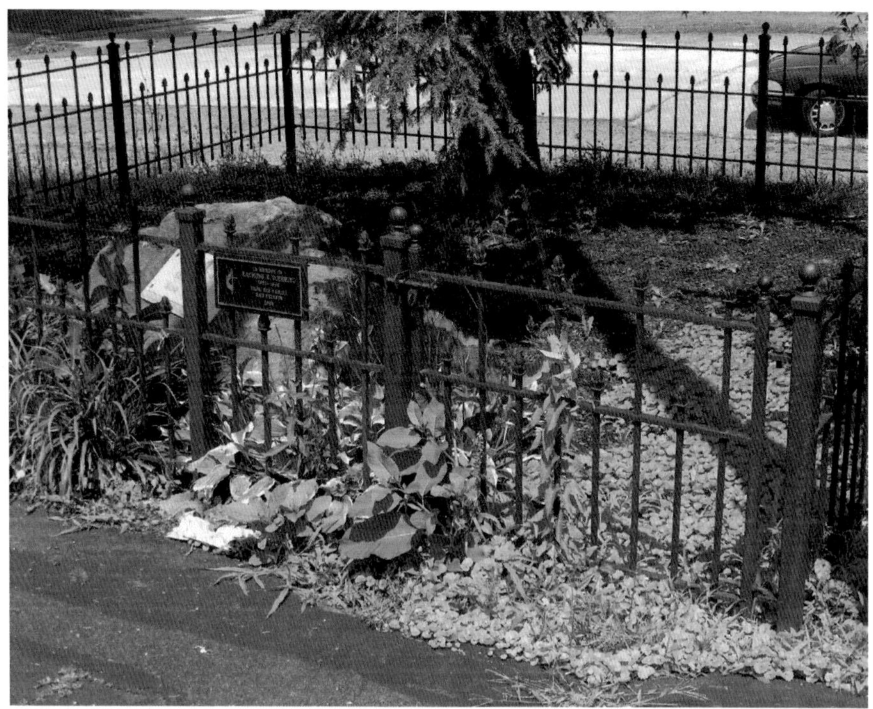

The Kellogg Family Cemetery now rests within a fenced-in area beside a parking lot in South Euclid. *Author's collection.*

build and maintain a fence around the Kellogg Family Cemetery (only a small part of the half-acre tract was used for burials.) Should they fail to do so, the deed would become "null and void."

The church did as it was asked and erected a fence around the small cemetery. The graveyard was even mentioned in an article from the *Plain Dealer* in 1941.

Today, the Kellogg Family Cemetery exists as a small, fenced-in area on the north side of the parking lot of the former Hillcrest United Methodist Church on South Green Road in South Euclid. There exists only one marker to indicate that it was ever used as a burial ground. The marker does not appear as a tombstone but rather as a small boulder. Mounted to the boulder is a plaque dedicated to the memory of Ezra Kellogg and his daughter Maria Ingram. There is no mention of the other four people who are likely buried there. It might be that Ezra's and Maria's stones were the only ones that remained when the boulder was placed.

19

PAYNE FAMILY CEMETERY

NO TRACE REMAINS

Lat 41°34'48.403" N, long 81°30'43.301" W
41.580112, -81.512028
Status: Fully Accessible

The story of the Payne family begins in Chatham, Middlesex County, Connecticut, with the August 1, 1787 marriage of Amasa Payne and Chloe Hopson. Five children were born to this union: two sons, Asahel and Amasa Harvey, and three daughters, Phebe, Emaline and Chloe. Sadly, Emaline and Chloe died in infancy.

In 1806, Phebe married Joel Randall, and within a few years, the two became prominent members of the local Congregationalist church. In 1818, they were sent west to Ohio, where they were instrumental in founding a church of the same denomination in Euclid. The following year, Phebe's parents; her brothers, Amasa Harvey and Asahel; and Asahel's wife, Lucy, joined Phebe and Joel. The family settled on a tract of land just to the east of Euclid Creek Village on what is now Euclid Avenue.

Tragedy struck the family on February 24, 1821, with the sudden passing of thirty-year-old Phebe Payne Randall. A small piece of land was cleared just to the east of the house, close to the road, where Phebe's remains were interred, thus establishing the Payne Family Cemetery. Four years later, while visiting a friend named Stephen Meeks in Vermilion, Joel Randall passed away quite unexpectedly. His remains were returned to Euclid, where he took his repose beside his late wife.

In 1836, Amasa Harvey Payne found a bride in Polly Farr of Euclid, and the two raised their children on this family farm. In 1841, the family patriarch, Amasa Payne, passed. His wife, Chloe Hopson Payne, joined him five years later. Both were interred in the small family cemetery. Ten years after his father's passing, Asahel Payne was buried beside his parents. His wife, Lucy, followed him to the grave a few years later, as did Phebe and Joel Randall's daughter Catherine.

The last burials there were Reuben S. Payne in 1861 and Reuben's fourteen-year-old daughter, Theresa, in 1863. Reuben was Amasa Harvey Payne's cousin and, at the time of his passing, lived three houses to the east of the Payne farm. He owned eighty acres of farmland and was employed as a ship's carpenter. A year after Theresa Payne's passing, Reuben's widow purchased a plot at the newly opened Euclid Cemetery and had the remains of her husband and daughter relocated to that burial ground, where they now lie in section D3.

Today, the Payne Family Cemetery exists as a grassy field just to the east of a wooded lot on the north side of Euclid Avenue across from Beverly Hills Drive. No trace of this early pioneer cemetery exists today, as all tombstone evidence has vanished.

20

JOHNSON/DEVOE FAMILY CEMETERY

IN A EUCLID PARK

Lat 41°36'04.244" N, long 81°30'37.385" W
41.601179, -81.510385
Status: Fully Accessible

Abraham Johnson Jr. was born in Pennsylvania in 1791 but didn't remain in his home state for very long. When the United States declared war on Great Britain on June 18, 1812, Abraham was one of the first to enlist. He signed up eleven days later as a corporal with the New York Militia and was placed in Captain James Cronk's company of Lieutenant Colonel Hugh W. Dobbins's regiment. During his six months of service, Corporal Johnson served the majority of his duty along the Niagara Frontier. The most noted of these actions was the Battle of Queenston Heights, the first major battle of the War of 1812, which occurred on October 13 of that year.

Following his service, Abraham Johnson Jr. remained in New York, where he met and married Sarah Ann DeVoe, daughter of Benjamin and Letitia Holmes DeVoe. Following the death of Sarah's father in 1819, the Johnsons set out for Ohio and arrived in 1822. Five years later, they continued on and settled in the northern end of Euclid Township. There, Abraham and Sarah raised their family.

Sarah's younger brother, Luke B. DeVoe, made the trip from New York to Ohio with them. In Euclid, on July 4, 1838, Luke wed Maria Crosier, daughter of Jason and Almira Crosier. The DeVoes lived on a farm located just to the north of the land occupied by Abraham and Sarah Johnson.

On February 22, 1843, Abraham Johnson Jr. purchased the farm that he and his family had been residing on for the last fifteen years. It consisted of 101 acres and was purchased at the cost of three dollars per acre. The previous owners of this property, their landlords, were Frederick Norton, Joshua Coit and Robert Foster, all of New York City.

In the years that followed, the Johnsons lost two members of their family and established a small cemetery on their property. The burial ground was located just to the north of the barn and on the west bank of a stream that bisected the property. One son and one daughter died sometime between 1840 and 1850 and were interred there. Edward DeVoe, son of Luke and Maria, also died during this time. He was buried beside his cousins.

Finding more opportunities to the west, the Johnsons decided to sell their farm and move on to Michigan. The new owners were Phidelia and Nathaniel P. Glazier, who purchased the farm, now comprising eighty-nine and a half acres, on June 23, 1854. Reserved from this sale were five square rods of land, approximately thirty-six feet by thirty-six feet, which were being used as the burying ground. From Euclid, the Johnsons pressed on to Cascade, Kent County, Michigan, where Sarah Ann DeVoe Johnson passed

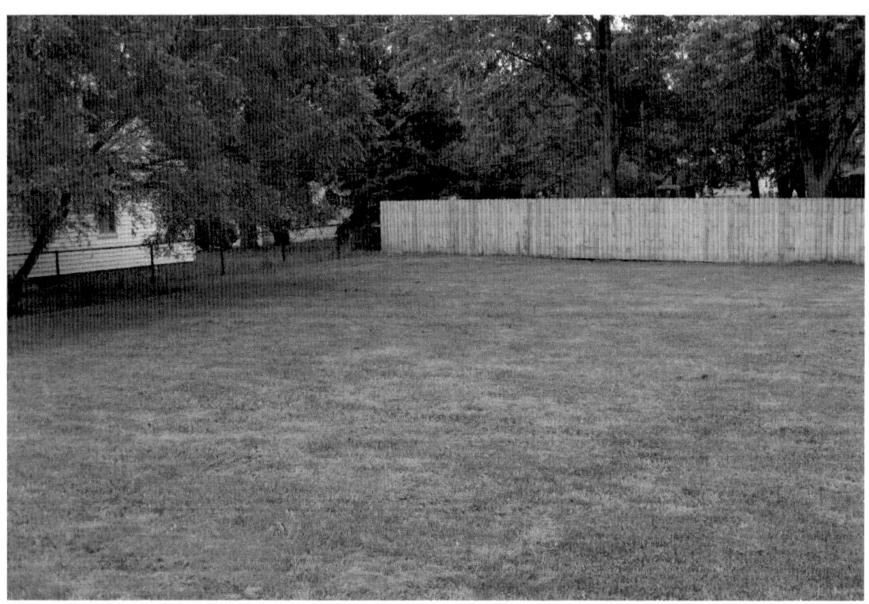

Buried somewhere beneath the northeast corner of Russell Avenue Park in Euclid lie the remains of the Johnson and DeVoe families. *Author's collection.*

away on May 3, 1859. Abraham Johnson Jr. followed her just six years later. Both are interred at Daniels Cemetery in Caledonia, Michigan.

The next to be buried in the Johnson/DeVoe Cemetery was Luke DeVoe, who died in 1856 at the age of forty-four. His youngest son, Edgar, was the last person known to be buried there. Edgar DeVoe died in 1857 at the age of five.

Title transfers of this land following the Johnson sale do not mention this little cemetery, though it appears in a few county atlases. It last appeared in 1903, when it was in the hands of John and Catherine Sulcer. The little cemetery was maintained through the 1940s and was left primarily undisturbed by the 1950s housing development that went on in that area.

The best estimates place this tiny burying ground somewhere along the northeast edge of Russell Avenue Park. Identifying landmarks, such as the barn and stream, are long gone. The barn was torn down many years ago, and the stream was rerouted and now runs through a culvert. No gravestones can be located in Euclid Cemetery, and no reinterment records for the Johnsons or DeVoes exist. It is likely that they are all still interred on this site. The tombstones might have fallen over and sunk beneath the surface of the grass, or it might be that they were removed by the city or fell victim to vandals. Only future surveys of the park property will yield answers.

PART II

SOUTHEAST CEMETERIES

SOUTHEAST CUYAHOGA COUNTY CEMETERIES WITH ORIGINAL TOWNSHIPS, CIRCA MID-1800s

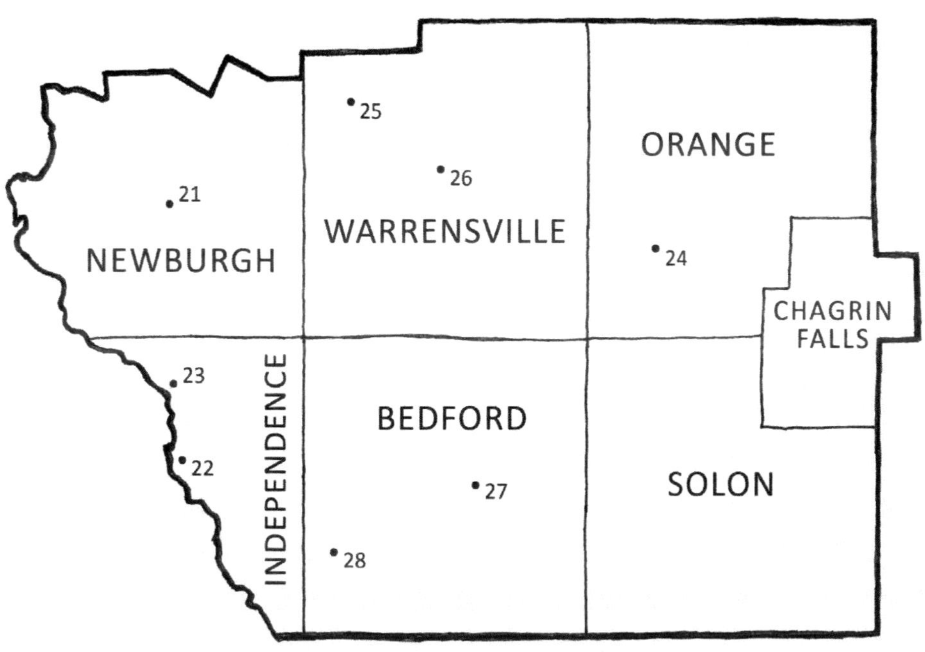

21. Newburgh Cemetery
22. Old Rockside Cemetery
23. Fosdick/Green Cemetery
24. Lander Road Cemetery
25. Shaker Graveyard
26. Warrensville Center Cemetery
27. Old Bedford Burying Ground
28. Gleeson Homestead Cemetery

21
NEWBURGH CEMETERY

AXTELL STREET BURYING GROUNDS

Lat 41°27'22.946" N, long 81°37'52.007" W
41.456374, -81.631113
Status: Partially Accessible

As Cleveland was first being settled in the late 1790s, so too was the township of Newburgh just to the south. Both competed for the distinction of being the county seat, and although the population of Newburgh was slightly higher, Cleveland won the contest. Though the mortality rate from diseases such as malaria was much lower south of the city, deaths were still commonplace among pioneer communities, and a cemetery was eventually needed.

The Newburgh Cemetery was first established around 1804 along the southern end of Newburgh Township lot 447 on what was first called Cemetery Street, later named Axtell Street. Originally comprising four acres, it expanded to encompass just over eight acres by the early 1870s. The earliest burials were those of the Burk and Miles families.

Another notable buried there was Alonzo Carter, the eldest child of Major Lorenzo Carter, who had sold the land for the cemetery to the township. It was also the resting place for six veterans of the American Revolution, three veterans of the War of 1812 and nearly thirty Union soldiers from the Civil War.

As the years progressed, Newburgh Township was slowly annexed, one section at a time, by the City of Cleveland. In December 1873, the section that contained the old Newburgh Cemetery was also absorbed.

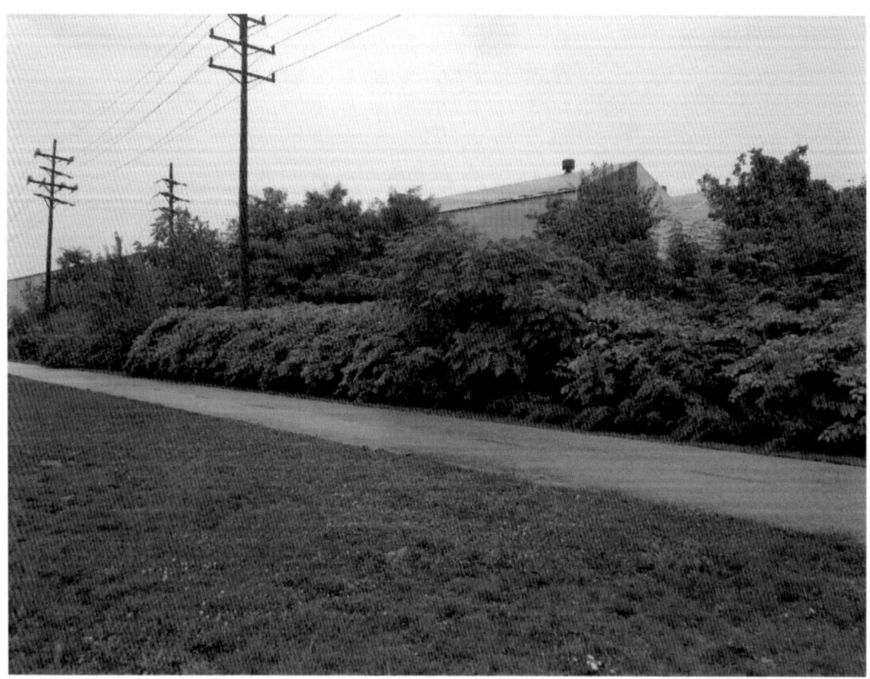

The Morgana Run Trail, which follows the route of the old Connotton Valley Railroad, crosses the former site of the Newburgh Cemetery. *Author's collection.*

With burials in this cemetery becoming less frequent, the City of Cleveland decided that it was time to put the land to better use. The area had already become a burgeoning industrial area, and few people wished to see their loved ones interred beside a steel mill. As it was, rail access to these mills and foundries was quite limited.

Thus, on July 18, 1881, the Cleveland city council granted the Connotton Valley Railroad (CVRR, later called the Wheeling and Lake Erie Railroad) permission to extend a rail line through the western end of the cemetery. For this land right, CVRR president Francis Bartlett paid $16,500. But what would become of those interred in what was now known as the Axtell Street Cemetery? The answer was simple.

Just to the west was located the farm of Isaac Reid, an early Newburgh resident, who had plenty of land to spare. On August 26, 1881, Reid sold twenty acres of his farmland to the City of Cleveland for $10,000. This property became the new Harvard Grove Cemetery.

Plans for moving the graves were posted in the Axtell Street Cemetery office for public viewing, and family members of those buried in unmarked graves were asked to come and indicate their loved ones' places of interment. The problem with this was that many of these families were gone, either deceased or moved away, and there was hardly anyone left to identify them. Exhumations began in November of that year.

When the grim task was complete, approximately three thousand bodies were moved from Axtell Street to Harvard Grove. It should be noted that only graves with headstones or those that were fortunate enough to be identified by a family member or friend were moved. Everyone else interred there was left behind. Following the final relocation from Axtell Street, Harvard Grove Cemetery was officially opened. The first official burial at the new cemetery took place on January 2, 1882, with the interment of forty-four-year-old Frederick Herrington of Haddock Street.

Though the Axtell Street Cemetery was now "officially" cleared, it continued to be a nuisance. As late as 1885, area residents were still complaining about the state of the former burial ground. Apparently, the City of Cleveland was rather relaxed on the matter of filling in the holes that, until recently, had been occupied by the dead. After many complaints, the remaining $6,500 from the sale of the cemetery to CVRR, which had been set aside for the removal of the bodies, was tapped, and the holes were ultimately filled in.

With the exception of the railroad and a switching yard for trains, the land that had been occupied by the Axtell Street Cemetery sat relatively untouched for about the next twenty-five years. It wasn't until June 20, 1906, that Francis Bartlett sold the balance of this lot to the Union Rolling Mills Company, which had an eye on it for future expansion. This addition to the mill began in early 1909, and more graves were unearthed.

Several tombstones, a larger number of bones and even a human skull were discovered during this excavation. Among the items found was the almost perfectly preserved sandstone grave marker of a veteran of the American Revolution that had served with the Massachusetts Militia. The stone was located under three feet of soil and read:

In
Memory of
Jeddidiah Hubbel Esq.
who died
June 11, 1813
aged 82 years

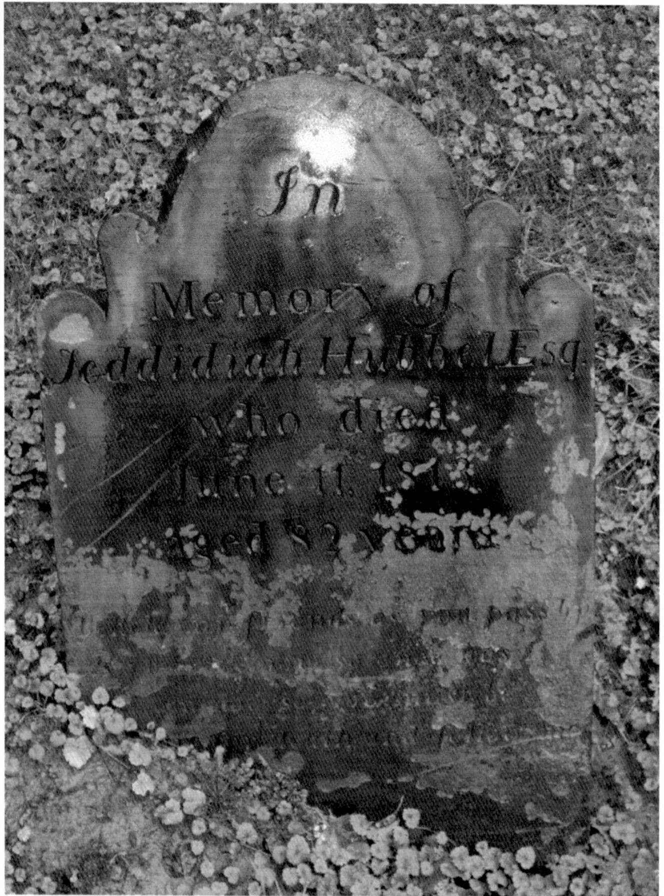

The headstone of Jeddidiah Hubbel now rests at Harvard Grove Cemetery. *Author's collection.*

Following the excavation, the tombstones and remains were removed to Harvard Grove Cemetery. Whatever else wasn't uncovered during the mill expansion was left undisturbed and still remains there.

Today, much of the site sits on the grounds of Jemison Demsey Metals and is a partially graveled lot behind the main building. The western edge of the old cemetery is accessible along the Morgana Run Trail (the former route of the Connotton Valley Railroad) between Marble Avenue and Aetna Road. Most of the cemetery grounds, the part that likely still contains the remains of some of Newburgh's earliest pioneers, are located just to the east of the fence on private property.

22
OLD ROCKSIDE CEMETERY

HARPER FAMILY BURIAL GROUND

Lat 41°23'41.082" N, long 81°37'29.697" W
41.394745, -81.624916
Status: Fully Accessible

Barely a trace remains of this early graveyard, located on Old Rockside Road, just east of Canal Road in Valley View. It was established on a 110-acre farm that was purchased by John I. Harper in 1816. Harper came to the area from New York with his wife, Amanda Rudd, and brother Archibald—who died in 1825, possibly the first burial in the cemetery.

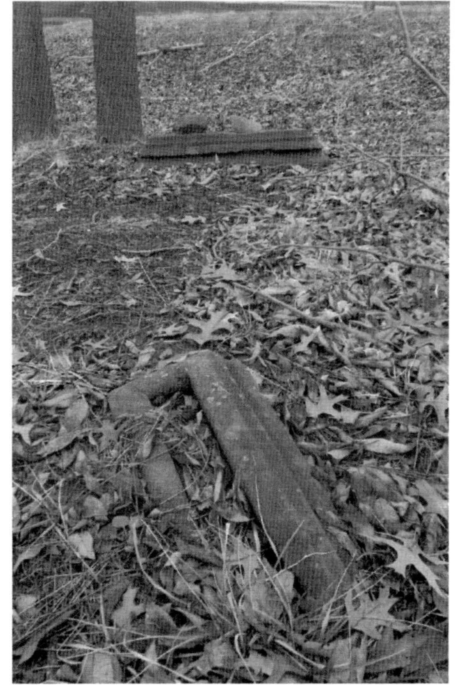

Two tombstone bases are all that remains of the Old Rockside Cemetery. *Author's collection.*

It has been reported that this cemetery is the final resting place for nearly one hundred individuals, many of whom were canal builders who died of swamp fever in 1827. It is also the burial place of Orange McArthur, a canal boat captain and constable of Independence Township, who died in 1837 at the age of twenty-six.

In 1929, only four headstones remained. One belonged to Captain McArthur, another to John I. Harper, one to Harper's five-year-old granddaughter Martha and one dedicated to the memory of Ithraim and Samantha Joiner, who died in the 1840s. Over the years, urban sprawl has taken its toll, and only the bases of two headstones remain—the ones for John and Amanda Harper. The rest of the tombstones have fallen over and are now buried or have been paved over by a parking lot and Old Rockside Road.

The cemetery now exists as a small, fenced-off area outside of the office building at 8300 Old Rockside Road. The Village of Valley View rededicated the remains of the little burial ground on April 26, 2003.

23

FOSDICK/GREEN CEMETERY

THE HOUSE FLANKED BY HEADSTONES

Lat 41°24'15.263" N, long 81°37'35.502" W
41.404240, -81.626528
Lat 41°24'16.014" N, long 81°37'35.698" W
41.404448, -81.626583
Status: Fully Accessible

The story of the Fosdick Green Cemetery is a confusing one and quite unique, to say the least. It was, in fact, composed of two separate burial grounds located on the same property and within paces of each other.

The official story that appears in early county histories claims that Jeremiah Fosdick settled on a hill that overlooked the Cuyahoga River Valley. In 1827, he relocated to the bottomlands and built a two-and-a-half-story sandstone house with his sons. Eventually, most of the land was sold to a man named Green, whose daughter had married one of the Fosdick boys. Historical records, however, point to the contrary.

William Green and his wife, Hepsibeth, had come to Ohio from Massachusetts around 1815 and first settled in Brecksville. Five years later, they removed to eastern Independence, then part of Newburgh Township, and settled in a small village that was then known as Shepard. In 1830, Green purchased a forty-acre tract and built the impressive stone house that stood on that site. On Independence Day 1847, William Green's daughter, Emily, married Moses Quimby Fosdick, son of Henry

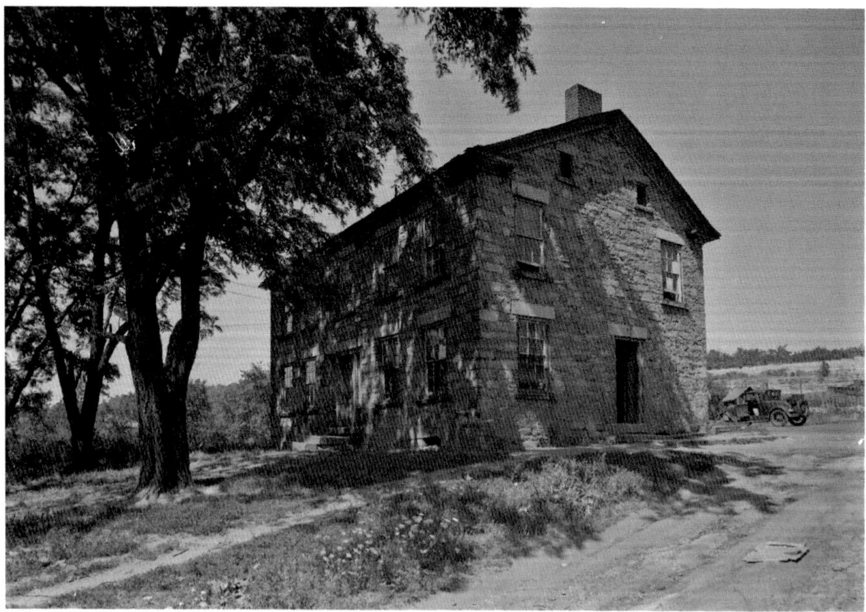

The Fosdick House on Canal Road. Just out of view are the two burial sites that flanked the home. *Library of Congress.*

Crawford Fosdick (not Jeremiah) of Tuscarawas County. In fact, Moses was the first of the Fosdicks to live in Cuyahoga County.

Following the death of William Green in early 1865, Moses and Emily Fosdick continued to occupy the old Green homestead. It remained in their family for the next few generations.

As to the burial plots located on the grounds, the first was located 30 feet north of Fosdick Road and 20 feet east of Canal Road. Immediately north of this sat the grand sandstone house. On the north side of the house, 140 feet north of Fosdick and 30 feet east of Canal, sat the other burial plot. It was rumored that, as with the Old Rockside Cemetery, these were originally the burial sites of canal builders who had died from fever. Also buried here were William and Hepsibeth Green and descendants of the Fosdick family.

In 1960, the land was sold to the Norton Construction Company, which was going to erect an office building on the site. Furthermore, the company wished to use the dirt on the grounds for fill on other projects. The problem was that the grounds were still occupied by the cemeteries. The civic league of Valley View set itself to the task of determining if anyone was, in fact, still buried in either of the two plots. One still contained a large obelisk for the Fosdick family, but not even the descendants of the Fosdicks knew if the graves were occupied.

The sandstone house was raised that year, and construction commenced. It is stated that the graves that could be located were removed to Maple Shade Cemetery on the northeast corner of Rockside and Brecksville Roads, but no such monument for the Fosdick family exists at that cemetery. Today, the former burial plots are located on the front lawn of the office building at 5811 Canal Road in Valley View.

24
LANDER ROAD CEMETERY

ARNOLD FAMILY GRAVEYARD

Lat 41°26'41.755" N, long 81°27'49.158" W
41.444932, -81.463655
Status: Partially Accessible

Located on the property that sits on Lander Road, just two addresses north of Smithfield Road in Orange, is what was once known as the Lander Road Cemetery. It was approximately a quarter of an acre in size and sat on the northeast corner of the lot, just north of a small creek that runs through the property. Henry and Mariah Arnold—who on September 26, 1829, had purchased a forty-acre farm there from Isaiah and Lydia Austin—established the burying ground.

Henry was quite young at the time, only twenty-two. He was born in 1807 in Berkshire, Massachusetts, to Elijah and Annis Graham Arnold. He had come to Ohio with his parents and his brother, Elestus, just before he had made his purchase. The entire family settled in the immediate area, primarily close to the corner of Lander and Jackson Roads. It is widely believed that the Arnold home was used as a stop on the Underground Railroad.

Henry and Mariah Arnold owned this property for just over six years before selling it in 1835 and relocating to Michigan, where Mariah Arnold passed away ten years later. It should be noted that the cemetery ground was not included in the sale of the farm. The cemetery remained in the Arnold family well into the twentieth century.

The next owner to possess the farm for a significant length of time was Jonah P. Hill, who held the land from 1836 to 1840. John Calvert Bleasdale, an Englishman by birth, took custody of the land for the next ten years until he sold it to Joel S. Giles. It stayed in the Giles family until it was sold to Maurice and Susan Roberts on October 19, 1867. It was sold again to Alvin Burgess in 1884.

There were many more owners throughout the late nineteenth and early twentieth centuries, though the Jones family purchased it in 1923. They had grander ideas in mind. Incidentally, this was the last time that any mention of the little quarter-acre "grave-yard" appeared in title transfers concerning the land. It had existed for nearly one hundred years before passing into oblivion. Emily P. Jones purchased the land outright in 1930 and began to subdivide the property.

The original burials that took place there were likely those of Henry and Mariah Arnold's children who died in infancy. After they moved to Michigan, the cemetery passed to Henry's brother, Elestus Arnold. Five other burials are known to have taken place there. Three of Elestus's sons lost their wives early on. Hannah Tucker, wife of Douglas T. Arnold, passed

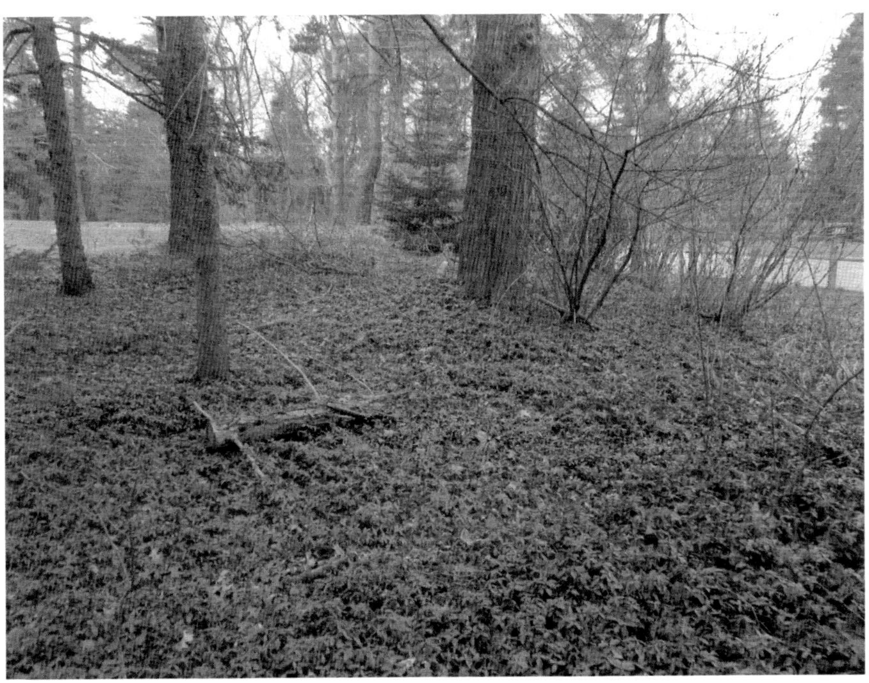

A myrtle-covered patch marks the site of the old Lander Road Cemetery. *Author's collection.*

away on September 9, 1861, at the age of thirty-five. Nancy R. Dunwell, the first wife of Collins Arnold, died on July 3, 1846, at twenty-five years of age. The most tragic loss was the passing of Jane N. Smith, the twenty-three-year-old wife of Ralph Arnold. She died on February 3, 1836, just nineteen days after giving birth to their daughter, Lillie. Furthermore, she passed the day before what would have been her and Ralph's first wedding anniversary. The other two burials that took place there were Henry and Elestus's parents, Elijah and Annis Graham Arnold. Annis died on January 18, 1860, at the age of seventy-seven. Her husband passed away at the age of eighty-nine, seven years to the day after his wife.

The eastern part of the cemetery is now located under the western edge of Lander Road, as the street was widened many years ago. Also, a storm drain was installed on the verge of the road, which occupies even more of the old cemetery. The balance of the burying ground rests just beyond a stand of tall hedges on the side of the road at the front of the property. Here, the ground is very uneven and is covered in creeping myrtle. The northern end of the old burial ground sits under a driveway for this residence. The graves that could be located within this cemetery were removed in 1936 to Mount Hope Cemetery on the corner of Miles and Harper Roads. No grave marker for Elijah Arnold could be located in this cemetery, and no trace of the old Lander Road Cemetery remains today.

25
SHAKER GRAVEYARD

INITIALS AND DATES

Lat 41°29'02.284" N, long 81°34'04.112" W
41.483968, -81.567809
Status: Partially Accessible

The Shaker Community of North Union was formed in the area that is now Shaker Heights in 1822. Three families made up the settlement—the Mill family, the Middle family and the Gathering family. The old Shaker Graveyard was established on a small piece of land, about eighty feet by eighty feet in size, at the corner of an apple orchard that was closest to the Middle family settlement along Lee Road. It was a quiet, serene place shaded by willows and evergreens. Most of the tombstones were little more than small, roughly quarried stones that bore only the person's initials and the date of his or her death. Others were simple, wooden markers, and a few of the grave sites even sat unmarked.

Due to a lack of interest in the teachings of the Shakers, the community slowly dwindled until only twenty-seven members remained. In 1889, the settlement disbanded and relocated to the settlement of the Whitewater Shakers in southwest Ohio. Three years later, the land was sold to the Shaker Heights Land Company, which began to develop the property. In 1895, South Park Boulevard was laid out.

While grading the land for the road, construction workers uncovered the tombstone of Revolutionary War veteran Jacob Russell (1746–1821), the father of the community's founder, Ralph Russell. Jacob Russell's headstone was moved to a nearby hillside on South Park Boulevard, and construction

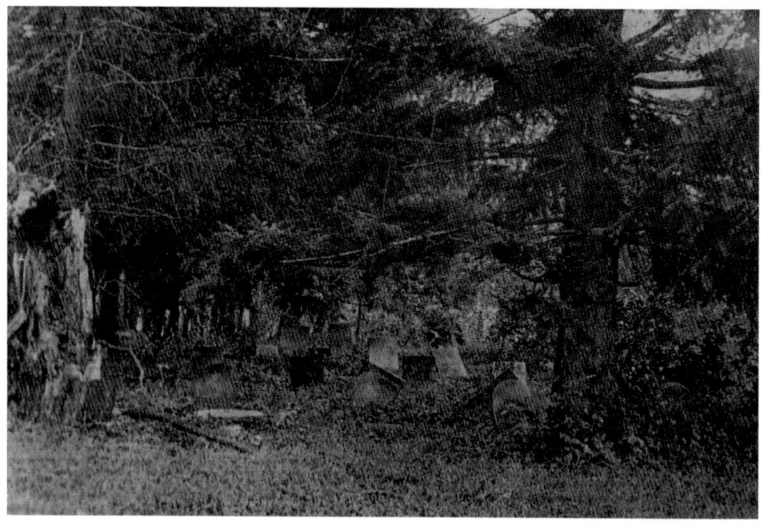

The abandoned Shaker Graveyard rests in the shade of willows and evergreens, circa 1905. *Cleveland Public Library*.

continued. His remains were never searched for and are presumably still located under South Park Boulevard.

In 1905, the land was sold to the Van Sweringen brothers, who continued to develop the community of Shaker Heights. Four years later, 89 bodies were relocated from the old Shaker Graveyard to Warrensville West Cemetery. The problem is that there were more than 130 people buried there, meaning that close to 50 sets of remains were left behind. Those who were moved were interred in a mass grave marked by a boulder. A plaque on the marker restates the words of Shaker founder Ann Lee:

> *Do all your work as though*
> *you had a thousand years to live,*
> *and as you would if you knew*
> *you must die tomorrow.*

The site of the old Shaker Graveyard is partially located under a little clump of trees and a mulched flowerbed, between the fourth and fifth houses on the south side of South Park Boulevard just west of Lee Road. As this part of the cemetery rests on private property, it is strictly off limits. The balance rests beneath that section of South Park Boulevard itself and is fully accessible to the public.

26

WARRENSVILLE CENTER CEMETERY

OLD EAST VIEW GRAVEYARD AND VAULT

Lat 41°27'59.483" N, long 81°21'23.839" W
41.466523, -81.536622
Status: Fully Accessible

Very little is known concerning this burial ground, which once sat near the northwest corner of Warrensville and Kinsman Roads (now Warrensville Center Road and Chagrin Boulevard) between a tavern and an old steam sawmill. For many years, the land was the property of Dyer Sherman, an early area pioneer. Following Sherman's death from numb palsy in 1850, half an acre was contracted out to Willard R. Green for unspecified reasons. By 1858, the balance of this lot was in the hands of Frederick and Minerva Welton. Maps contemporary with that time period show an area marked off, about half an acre along Warrensville Road just to the north of the tavern.

By the 1870s, the land belonged to Joseph and Caroline Keller. On May 21 of that year, Mr. and Mrs. Keller sold the half-acre lot on the northeast corner of their land to the trustees of Warrensville Township for $500. The township erected a stone burying vault on the property. The main room of this vault was buried beneath a small, grass-covered mound, while the façade bore the year of construction above the door.

From then on, the site appeared on maps and atlases as a cemetery or simply as the property of the township trustees. It was also mentioned as being a cemetery in a title transfer that occurred in 1904, when an adjoining piece of land was sold to the Shaker Lakes and Boulevard Railroad, the early forerunner of the Shaker Rapid.

During the early 1900s, this area of Warrensville Township became the village of East View. In 1911, East View made an attempt to break off entirely from Warrensville and become its own township. This was because Warrensville was charging its residents high road assessments for road improvements. East View was almost successful in breaking off but was ultimately blocked by the county because the village also encompassed the town hall and cemetery. Had it been able to break away, East View would have gotten these properties, and Warrensville would have been left with nothing.

On March 8, 1916, the trustees of Warrensville Township sold the half-acre cemetery at public auction. Samuel J. Gibbs, the mayor of East View, paid $1,725 for the lot. He, in turn, sold it to the Van Sweringen Company three years later. By 1922, the trustees of the First Trust & Savings Company held the title for the land, and the lot was simply marked as containing "Vaults."

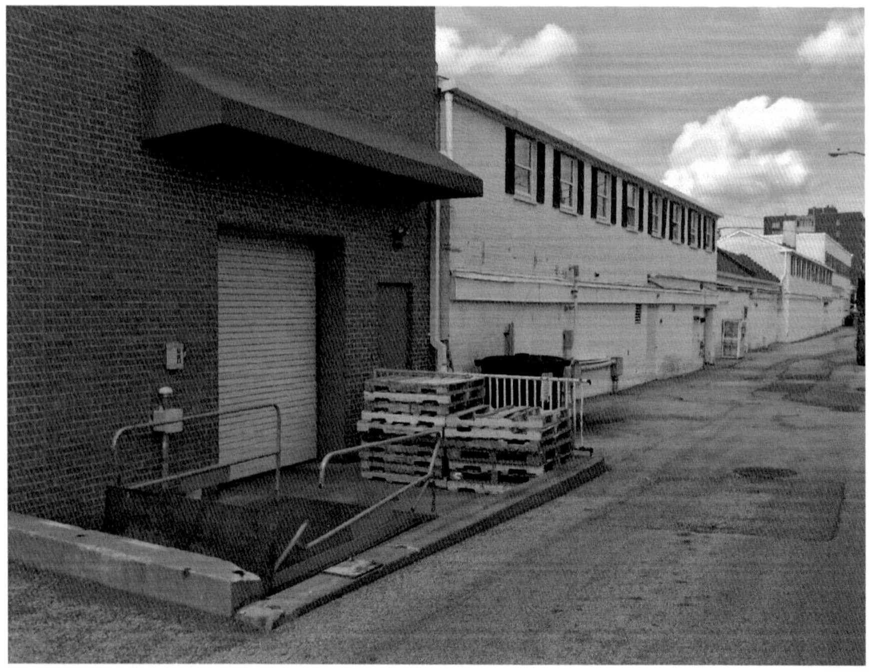

A loading dock now occupies the space once used as the Warrensville Center Cemetery and Vault. *Author's collection.*

In all actuality, there was only one vault on the property. The vault did not contain any permanent interments but was used to hold bodies during the winter months when snow covered the roads and graves could not be dug because of the frozen ground. The vault stood on that site until 1927, when it was decided that it would be torn down to make way for an extension of South Moreland Boulevard (now Van Aken Boulevard.)

It is unknown exactly how many people were buried on this small lot. Also unknown is who they were and what became of their remains. Today, the site rests along the west side of Warrensville Center Road between Chagrin Boulevard and Farnsleigh Road and is occupied by the northeast corner of a grocery store and loading dock.

27
OLD BEDFORD BURYING GROUND

A HORRIFYING DISCOVERY

Lat 41°23'15.382" N, long 81°31'42.168" W
41.387606, -81.528380
Status: Fully Accessible

Located on a sandy knoll on the north side of East Taylor Road between Washington Street and the north entrance to Bedford Cemetery once stood the Old Bedford Burying Ground. The first burial was that of Mary F. Bartlett, which occurred on September 26, 1808.

On March 13, 1832, the original property owners, Hezekiah and Clarissa Dunham, sold the land to Bedford Township for eight dollars. The land contained 0.9 acres and was forever to be occupied and used as a public burying ground. Twenty-five years later, however, a new cemetery was established just to the south on what is now Broadway Avenue, though the original one might still have been in use into the 1870s.

In January 1881, the process of leveling off the land of the old cemetery began. Three persons were exhumed—a man who had died of smallpox, another who had passed from cholera and a woman who, it was horrifyingly learned, had been buried alive; her body was turned over in her coffin and grotesquely contorted. Many sets of remains had been moved to the new cemetery in the years prior to this. These were the remains of early pioneers whose descendants had bought family lots at the new cemetery.

On May 11, 1881, the Village of Bedford sold the land to Martha L. Cowles and the Connotton Valley Railroad for a total of two dollars. The

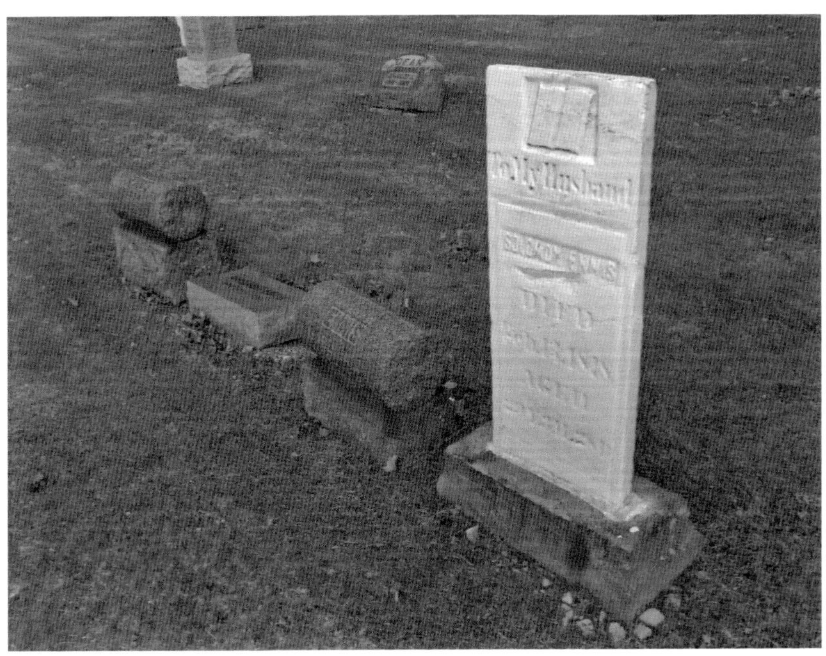

The old and the new. The tall white headstone of Solomon Ennis (right) now rests at the Bedford Cemetery beside those of his family members (left). *Author's collection.*

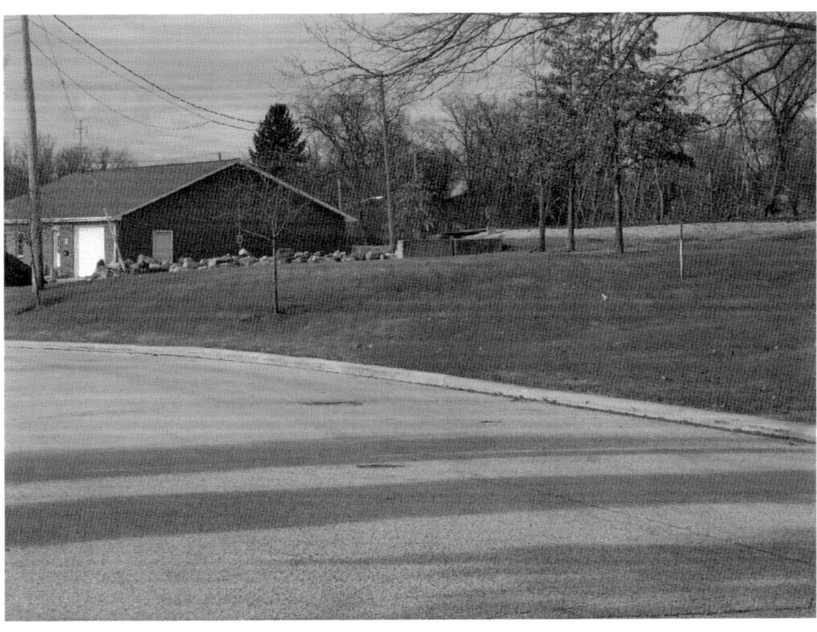

A grassy hillside along East Taylor Road marks the original site of the Old Bedford Burying Ground. *Author's collection.*

property was sold with the understanding that the new owners would remove and reinter all human remains found buried on the premises, as required by statute. The remains that could be found were relocated to a mass grave at the new cemetery.

Within a few years, the Connotton Valley Railroad was sent across the site, and by 1903, it was under the dominion of the Wheeling and Lake Erie Railroad. By 1914, there was no longer any mention on maps of a cemetery having been at that location. The land was now owned by E.L. Cowles as part of a 5.25-acre lot, originally owned by Martha L. Cowles.

Today, the site of the Old Bedford Burying Ground is a parking lot and a grassy patch with railroad tracks crossing the land. The building that sits to the west of the parking lot is just off the property.

28
GLEESON HOMESTEAD CEMETERY

EGYPT MOUND BURIAL PLOT

Lat 41°22'18.833" N, long 81°34'38.712" W
41.371898, -81.577420
Status: Accessible with Caution

On a windswept hilltop in Walton Hills sits one of the most desolate and haunting cemeteries in Cuyahoga County. Marked by a single grave and an ancient tree that resembles something out of a Tim Burton film, visitors find the Gleeson Homestead Cemetery. This mound, deep in the woods, once held a commanding view of the small village of Little Egypt far below. Since those early years, a dense forest has sprung up around it, isolating it from the rest of the modern world.

This story begins in 1812 with surveyor Moses Gleeson and his wife, Polly Richardson, of Stillwater, Saratoga County, New York, traveling to Stark County, Ohio, with their three children. Two years later, they continued on to Independence and ultimately settled in Bedford Township, where they added eleven more children to their family. It was there that Moses Gleeson built his homestead in the small village of Little Egypt along the east side of the old state road to Pittsburgh. He was very active throughout his life in farming and milling but also operated an inn and stagecoach stop, called the World's End Tavern, out of his house.

The small cemetery was first established on the mound behind the Gleeson homestead in 1833 with the passing of Rebecca Gleeson, an infant daughter of Moses and Polly. More than twenty years passed before it received another burial. Records concerning the location of the cemetery are confusing to say the least. Books available at the Western Reserve Historical Society incorrectly place it on Dunham Hill in Valley View, formerly Independence Township, which rests just to the northeast of the confluence of Tinkers Creek and the Cuyahoga River. These books further claim that the cemetery sat on "Carey property," and while these last statements might be true, the Dunham Hill and Carey property in question were in Bedford Township and not in Independence.

On April 4, 1848, Moses and Polly's son Edmund D. Gleeson married Charlotte Comstock. They had two children, Frank and Clara, and resided with the rest of the Gleeson family at the World's End Tavern. In 1851, Edmund Gleeson began construction on a fine stone residence on the hillside overlooking Canal and Tinkers Creek Roads, the site incorrectly referred to above as having contained the Gleeson Homestead Cemetery. This house was completed in early 1854, but Edmund did not enjoy it for very long. He passed away on October 26 of that year and was laid to rest in the family cemetery behind his father's house. Following his passing, a white limestone monument was placed over his grave.

The next burial to occur there was that of Edmond Richardson Gleeson, who died on October 1, 1864, just four days shy of his fifth birthday. Young Edmund was the son of Moses and Polly's son William. His name was added to the north face of his uncle Edmond's headstone.

These deaths were followed on May 8, 1867, by the passing of the family patriarch. It was at the death of Moses Gleeson that his surviving family officially reserved, surveyed and set apart the cemetery from the rest of the property. It was a trapezoidal piece of land measuring 107 feet long, 71 feet wide at one end and 38 feet wide at the other. Thus far, the site had been known by the names of Dunham Hill and Egypt Mound. A new name was now added to the list: Cemetery Hill. The borders of the burial ground were marked by apple trees that have long since fallen.

Moses's wife, Polly Richardson Gleeson, followed him up the hill three years later in 1870. Other interments in this cemetery include Edmund's brothers Sardis, in 1875; Charles, in 1880; William, in 1891; and Moses P. Gleeson, in 1892.

In 1872, the Gleeson homestead, with the exception of the cemetery, was sold to Thomas Houge, who farmed the land. All the while, Edmund Gleeson's now-grown daughter Clara continued to operate the World's End Tavern. It was there that Clara met Dominick Carey, of Canada, who was staying as a guest at the inn. Carey was employed as a railroad contractor and was the superintendent of Paige, Carey and Company, a firm that constructed railroad bridges. After a time, the two were wed and started a family of their own. Within just a few years, Dominck Carey and his brother, James, purchased the farm back from Thomas Houge. Clara kept up the inn while the Carey brothers operated a horse farm, called Maple Wood Stock Farm, on the vast tract of land on the west side of the road.

Sadly, Dominick Carey was killed quite unexpectedly in 1892. He drowned when a tramway he had been working on over a river in West Virginia collapsed. Upon his death, the farm passed to Clara and her children. Maple Wood Stock Farm was eventually sold to the Astor family and became the Astorhurst resort and country club. The old house, which had operated as the World's End Tavern for over a century, burned to the ground on November 29, 1941.

Soon after, the graves of the Gleeson family were moved to the Bedford Cemetery, not Maple Shade Cemetery in Independence, as some reports suggest. The graves of Edmund Gleeson and his infant sister Rebecca were left behind. Today, these lands are now a part of the Cleveland Metroparks Bedford Reservation in Walton Hills.

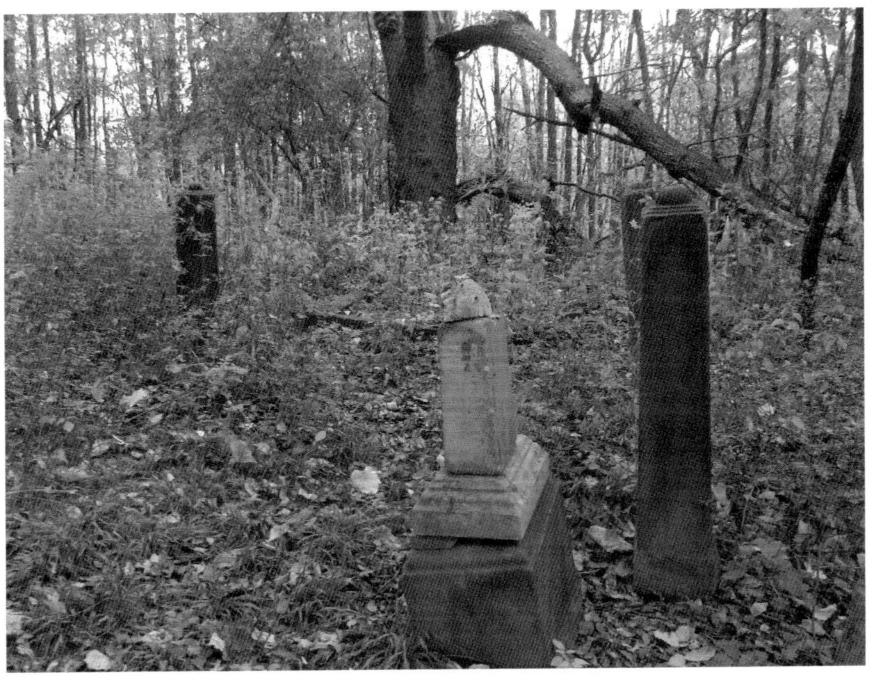

The lonely headstone of Edmund D. Gleeson stands watch from the top of Egypt Mound. *Author's collection.*

All that remains on the original cemetery site is the headstone for Edmund Gleeson, six sandstone posts and a small, stone-lined area that once held the remains of those who were buried there. Though Edmund Richardson Gleeson's name still appears on the same stone as his uncles, his remains were relocated to Bedford Cemetery with the rest of his family. Rebecca Gleeson's grave, though still on this site, is unmarked.

When visiting this site, it's best to park at the golf course on the west side of Dunham Road near Tinkers Creek Road. From there, carefully cross the road and proceed south on Dunham Road until the hill to your left is nearly even with the verge of the road. Just before a fire hydrant, a small trail leads to your left and into the woods. You will soon see scattered bricks on the forest floor. These are the ruins of the World's End Tavern. Continue to follow this broken trail to the north and east and keep walking until you reach the highest point of land in the area. There, you will discover all that remains of the Gleeson Homestead Cemetery.

Please use extreme caution when visiting this site. The terrain might be difficult for some to manage. Furthermore, you will have to fight through many thickets of pricker bushes to reach your destination.

PART III

SOUTHWEST CEMETERIES

SOUTHWEST CUYAHOGA COUNTY CEMETERIES WITH ORIGINAL TOWNSHIPS, CIRCA MID-1800S

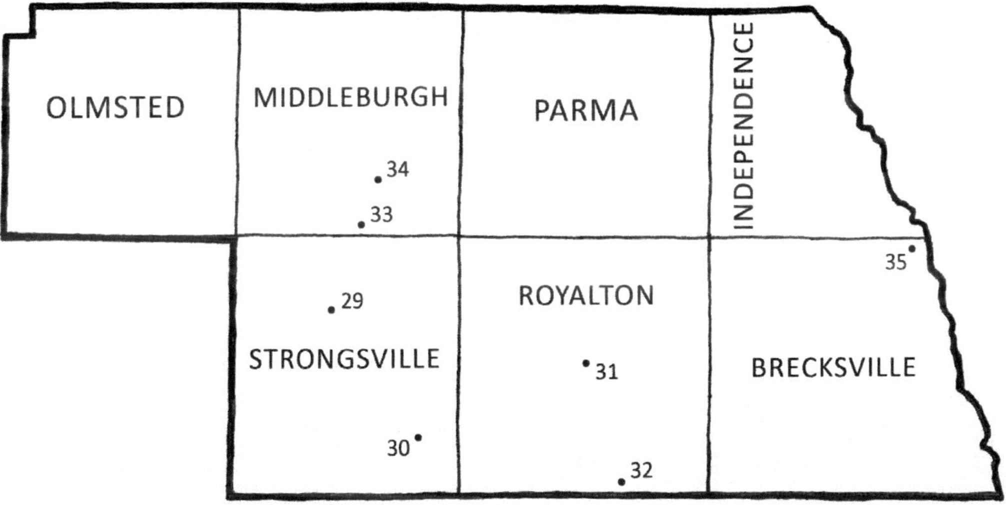

29. Strongsville Baptist Church Cemetery
30. Sanderson's Corners Cemetery
31. Old Royalton Burial Ground
32. Sarles Burial Ground
33. Lovejoy/Gardner/Fuller Cemetery
34. Gates Cemetery
35. Fitzwater Cemetery

29

STRONGSVILLE BAPTIST CHURCH CEMETERY

OLD ALBION BURIAL GROUND

Lat 41°19'46.852" N, long 81°50'10.478" W
41.329681, -81.836244
Status: Accessible with Caution

The small village of Albion once sat in the northern section of Strongsville Township. It was founded along the Columbus Turnpike (now Pearl Road) in 1834 by wool manufacturer Benjamin Northrup, who named it in honor of his hometown of Albion, New York. It existed as a thriving community until much of the village was destroyed by a fire in the late nineteenth century. Today, only small traces of Albion, such as a dam and an old road, remain.

Among these traces are the ruins of the Strongsville Baptist Church Cemetery. This story begins on February 9, 1841, with early residents Thaddeus and Betsy Lathrop selling sub-lots twenty and twenty-one in township lot fifty-three to the trustees of the newly organized First Baptist Society of Strongsville for $150. These trustees were Morris Pomeroy, John H. Whiting, Herman Leonard, Roswell Trask, Asher Selover, Edwin C. Marsh and Elias Combs. The total size of land was 1.62 acres.

A meetinghouse was immediately built on the site, close to present-day Pearl Road. The following year, a burial ground was established on the back half of these two sub-lots and was approximately 87 by 120 feet.

On July 10, 1873, by order of the Court of Common Pleas of Cuyahoga County, the First Baptist Church of Strongsville was forced to sell its assets.

The church was sold to the board of education of Strongsville for $200. Excluded from this sale was the burial ground, which was now fenced off. The church was used as a schoolhouse for the next twenty-four years until the property was sold to Castle Baker in May 1897. Though the church was no longer active, the cemetery was in use through the early 1900s.

The property changed hands quite a few times over the course of the next half century. The little fenced-in cemetery in the back was mentioned until 1959.

The majority of the burials there belonged to the Bosworth family. The earliest were John Bosworth (1760–1845), who served during the American Revolution with Elliott's Regiment of the Rhode Island Artillery, and his wife, Hannah Luther Bosworth (1769–1842), who is believed to be the first burial in this cemetery. There were at least seven other members of the Bosworth family buried there, the last being Sarah Mays Bosworth, the ninety-three-year-old widow of Benjamin Bosworth, John and Hannah's youngest son.

Evidence points to the entire Bosworth family, remains and headstones, being moved from the Baptist Church Cemetery to the Strongsville

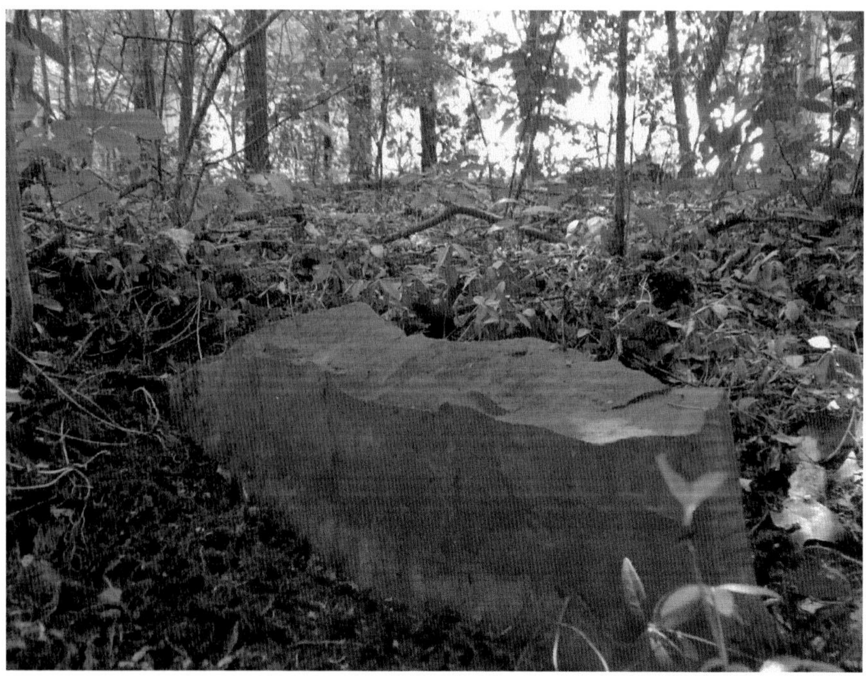

The fractured remains of a sandstone grave marker indicate that this was once the site of the Strongsville Baptist Church Cemetery. *Author's collection.*

Cemetery in April 1922. With the exception of Benjamin's first wife and his half brother Samuel, the entire family is now buried in section B, lot 22.

As for the old Baptist cemetery, the fence is long gone, and the burial ground is now a wooded lot behind the building at 11303 Pearl Road. The ground is fairly uneven and covered in creeping myrtle and tree roots. Though seemingly vacant, it yields a few surprises. Very close to the northwest corner of this lot are a few lonely sandstone blocks, tombstones that were broken off at their bases. The rest of these stones have probably sunk into the earth, hiding their vital information, though we do know what these epitaphs once read.

In 1929, the Daughters of the American Revolution transcribed the headstones. One grave was for Mary Ann, the wife of Thomas Lunn, who died on January 5, 1850, at the age of forty; the other was for Hannah Harris, who died on March 29, 1845, at the age of twenty-two. Hannah was the daughter of Russell Harris and Rosanna Bosworth, John's daughter. Two footstones also remained in the cemetery in 1929. One read "M.A.S." and the other read "L.C.S."

You should exercise extreme caution when visiting the ruins of this cemetery. Aside from the ground being uneven and the small broken tombstones that seem to appear out of nowhere, there is no fence to protect you from the one-hundred-foot cliff in the back of the property that drops to the Rocky River below.

30
SANDERSON'S CORNERS CEMETERY

A SMALL CEMETERY IN SOUTHEAST STRONGSVILLE

Lat 41°17'31.128" N, long 81°48'12.953" W
41.291980, -81.803598
Status: Strictly Off Limits!

This little burial ground was established on land belonging to Apollos R. Southworth Sr., probably during the 1820s or 1830s. Southworth was born on November 16, 1792, in Stoughton, Massachusetts, and served in the War of 1812, when he was stationed at Fort Warren near Boston. He first came to Strongsville in the autumn of 1816, stayed for a year and returned to Stoughton. The following February, he returned to Strongsville and remained there for the rest of his life. Shortly after his return, he dammed up a small creek, dug out a millpond and a short canal along a road that no longer exists and operated a mill where he manufactured furniture and wagons.

In 1820, Apollos Southworth married his first wife, Deborah Fisher, who died in 1869. Shortly after her passing, he married a woman named Lydia and continued to operate his mill. Apollos R. Southworth Sr. died in Strongsville on June 17, 1878, and was buried beside his first wife at the Strongsville Cemetery. His second wife, Lydia, joined them eleven years later.

In 1844, Apollos sold one acre to the Village of Strongsville, where a small red schoolhouse was built. This school also served as the community hall and center of religious gatherings. It was located just west of the creek and sat on the north side of what is now Drake Road across from Hunt Road.

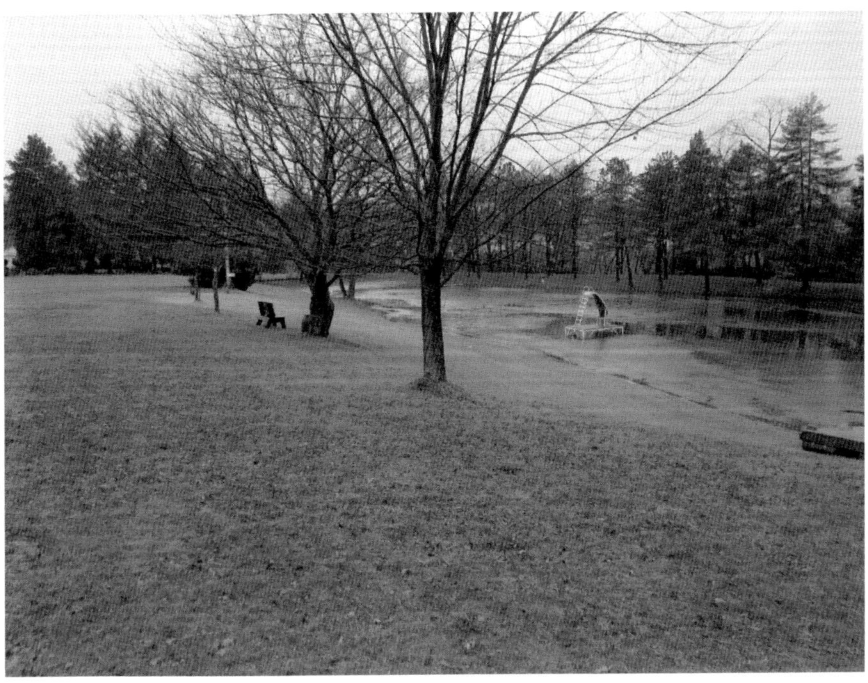

The east bank of the old millpond marks the site of the Sanderson's Corners Cemetery. *Author's collection.*

On the opposite bank of the creek, and about four hundred feet north of Drake Road, was a small burying ground that contained about twenty granite headstones. Buried there, among other unknown area residents, were two of Southworth's granddaughters—Mary Jane Sanderson (April 26, 1842 to November 3, 1847) and Lysander Sanderson (October 23, 1844 to March 5, 1854), daughters of Deborah Southworth and Samuel Sanderson.

When a new schoolhouse on a wedge of land between Drake and Hunt Roads replaced the little red one, the bodies from the small burying ground were moved to other cemeteries. Most are believed to have been reinterred in the cemetery at Bennett's Corners, about one mile to the southeast.

Still, the graves of these two children are not located at Strongsville Cemetery with the rest of their family or at Bennett's Corners Cemetery. They are likely still buried on the original site. The old cemetery grounds are now sitting on private property, a small park just to the east of the old millpond. This site is not accessible to the public.

31

OLD ROYALTON BURIAL GROUND

UPON THE VILLAGE GREEN

Lat 41°18'50.515" N, long 81°44'07.351" W
41.314032, -81.735375
Status: Fully Accessible

When Royalton Township was first settled in 1811, it was up to the newly arrived pioneers to inter their dead on their own lands. Such was the case of Catherine DePugh, the first wife of Charles Coates, who passed away shortly after their arrival and was buried somewhere on the old Coates Farm at Wallings Corners. Fourteen years passed before a township cemetery would be established, and that came by the hands of the Watkins family.

John Watkins was born in 1785 in Ashford, Winford County, Connecticut, to Jedidiah and Abigail Gould Watkins. In 1818, he arrived in Royalton Township with his wife, Beulah, and a brother named Cassina. Not long after, the Watkins family moved to the center of town. It was here, on May 11, 1825, that John and Beulah Watkins deeded five acres of land to the trustees of Royalton Township for the expressed purpose of establishing a burial ground, meetinghouses, a public square and other public buildings. It is believed, though, that the cemetery grounds had been used for such a purpose as early as 1822. John Watkins passed away in 1833, and his widow soon remarried Samuel Bosworth of Strongsville. She died in 1839 and was buried beside her first husband in the cemetery lands that they had deeded to the township.

Many notable citizens of Royalton were interred on this plot, including five veterans of the American Revolution. The most famous of these men was John Shepherd, who had also fought with George Washington during the French and Indian War. Shepherd is believed to have died at a more advanced age than any other veteran of both military actions. He died in 1847, just two and a half months shy of his 118th birthday.

As time progressed, many of the first settlers, originally buried on their own farms, were moved to the township burial ground, including Catherine DePugh Coates. By the 1860s, the cemetery was filling, and a new burial ground was sought. A suitable location was purchased from George Johnson in 1867 on the land adjoining the Disciple Church, and burials ceased at the old township cemetery.

By the late 1870s, the old burying ground had become so neglected that it was even described in a local book as being a "weed-choked and most unsightly spot." Realizing that the land could be put to better use, the township trustees proposed a bill to the statehouse to allow them to relocate the cemetery. This house bill (no. 363) passed on April 8, 1880, and gave

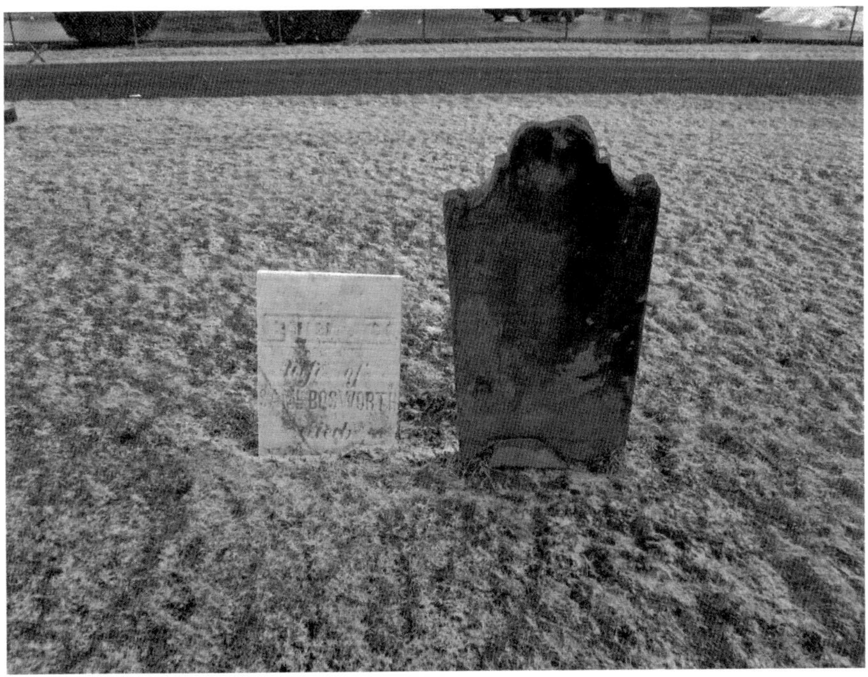

The headstones of John and Beulah Watkins, original owners of the Old Royalton Burial Ground, now stand side by side at North Royalton Cemetery. *Author's collection.*

authorization to use township funds and, if necessary, levy a tax to remove the bodies that remained in the abandoned burial ground. Thus, the graves were relocated to the new North Royalton Cemetery just to the east of the old burying ground. It has been said that a number of bodies were left behind and that these individuals had died of smallpox. In fact, that number is closer to two.

Today, a white gazebo marks the exact site of the cemetery on the southeast part of the village green. Some believe that the smallpox graves sit directly beneath it. When visiting North Royalton Cemetery, a number of headstones from the old burial ground are visible, primarily along the western edge of the grounds. Near the front of the cemetery is a white headstone with "Bulah, wife of Saml. Bosworth" written on it. Beside this stands an old sandstone grave marker, the epitaph completely worn away. Most likely, this is the headstone of Beulah's first husband, John Watkins, who had deeded the original cemetery lands to the township so many years ago.

32
SARLES BURIAL GROUND
THE SHORT-LIVED CEMETERY ON STATE ROAD

Lat 41°16'43.384" N, long 81°43'10.549" W
41.278718, -81.719597
Status: Partially Accessible

Jonathan Sarles was born on January 4, 1784, in Chappaqua, Westchester County, New York, to Isaiah Sarles and Anna Deane. It was here in this little hamlet, between the Hudson Valley and Connecticut, that he married Elizabeth "Betsey" Mace in 1809. In 1830, Jonathan Sarles traveled west to Ohio with his parents, wife, children and elder brother Samuel and settled in Royalton Township. Two years later, he purchased a three-hundred-acre tract of land from Simon Perkins for $800.

The first death in the family after arriving in Ohio was that of Adeline Ann Sarles, nineteen-year-old daughter of Samuel Sarles and Irena Stocking. She died on January 6, 1834. This is when a small family burial ground was established on the Sarles property.

On December 31, 1839, Jonathan and Betsey Sarles deeded two-thirds of an acre to the Township of Royalton for the cost of one dollar. This land was expressly to be used as a burying ground and for no other purpose. As a part of the agreement, the township was to keep it enclosed and bar all livestock, including cattle, horses and swine. Excluded from that list were sheep, which would be useful in keeping the grass short.

The next burial to take place there was Jonathan's wife, Betsey Mace Sarles, who died on September 6, 1844. Just over three months later, she was followed by Isaiah Sarles, Jonathan's father, who passed at age eighty-five. Isaiah was joined by his wife, Anna Deane Sarles, seven years later.

Jonathan Sarles died on July 8, 1853, and was interred beside his wife. Three years later, the small graveyard saw the interment of Almon Baxter Sarles, who died on October 5, 1854, just twenty-three days shy of his sixth birthday. Almon was the son of Jonathan and Betsey's youngest son, Arenzo. The last-known burial to take place there was that of Samuel Sarles, Jonathan's eldest sibling, who died on June 29, 1864, at the age of eighty-two. His headstone was marked with a Masonic insignia.

On April 11, 1883, the trustees of Royalton Township sold the piece of land to Frank Stupka for twenty-five dollars, thus breaking the agreement that it was always be used as a burying ground. In the title transfer, there is no mention of it ever having been used as a cemetery. It is most likely that the township trustees had the graves removed to North Royalton Cemetery and saw no need to retain the property.

At the North Royalton Cemetery, there is a section that contains the headstones of the Sarles family members who were originally buried in the small family graveyard. There is also a larger monument with the

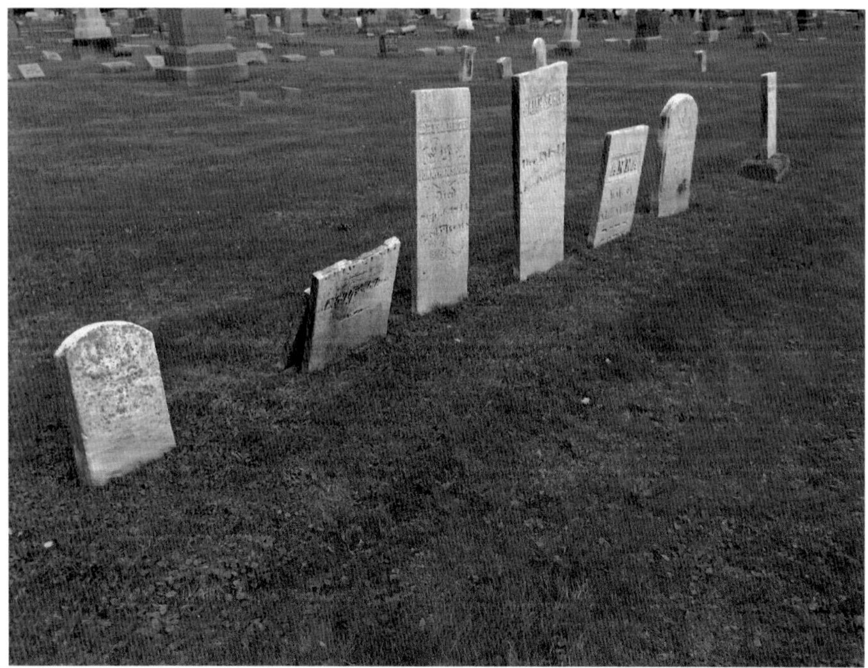

The graves of the Sarles family now located at North Royalton Cemetery. *Author's collection.*

name "Searles" on the base, a later spelling of the family name. The rest of the monument is completely worn away, and no specific names can be determined. Also completely illegible are two smaller headstones that rest among these graves. At the far south end of this section are two more small grave markers. Most of the vital information on them has been lost, but on close inspection, one bears the name "Samuel E." while the other seems to have the name "Fayette" engraved on it. These might have been neighbors or possibly other members of the Sarles family whose names have been scrubbed from history and time.

Today, the original site of the Sarles Burial Ground exists as a nondescript front yard on the west side of State Road in North Royalton. The southeast corner of this lot begins 630 feet north of the county line and continues northwest for another 122 feet. It originally extended into this property about 250 feet. However, as with most cemeteries that were once located along major thoroughfares, the road has been widened, and now the eastern edge lies beneath the verge of the southbound lane of State Road. That part is accessible to the public, while the balance, which rests on private property, is not. No trace of this cemetery exists today.

33

LOVEJOY/GARDNER/FULLER CEMETERY

SOLD TO MIDDLEBURGH TOWNSHIP AND LOST

Lat 41°21'08.258" N, long 81°49'31.598" W
41.352294, -81.825444
Status: Strictly Off Limits!

The story of this lost burial ground begins in 1819 with the arrival of a forty-two-year-old man from Windham, Vermont, named Solomon Lovejoy. Solomon had married Syrena Bitlis and settled in Fredonia, New York, where they raised a family. When he came to Ohio, he brought his wife and children with him and settled in the southern part of what was then called Middleburgh Township. Among his children was a twelve-year-old son named Ammy.

Shortly after the Lovejoy family came to Middleburgh, the Paul Gardner family, also from New York State, joined them. Paul and his wife, Isabel, had many children. One of these was a son named Amos, who was married to a woman named Sally.

The year 1832 saw the marriage of Ammy Lovejoy to a seventeen-year-old girl named Hanna Humaston, a daughter of Patrick Humaston Sr. A year later, the neighborhood grew just a little larger with the arrival of Jeremiah D. Fuller of Vermont. Soon after settling in Middleburgh, Fuller found a wife in Roxy Sprague.

With all of this growth in the community, it was only a matter of time before the neighborhood began to experience loss. The first occurred on December 8, 1836, with the death of Hanna Humaston Lovejoy's sister-in-law, Drusilla, who

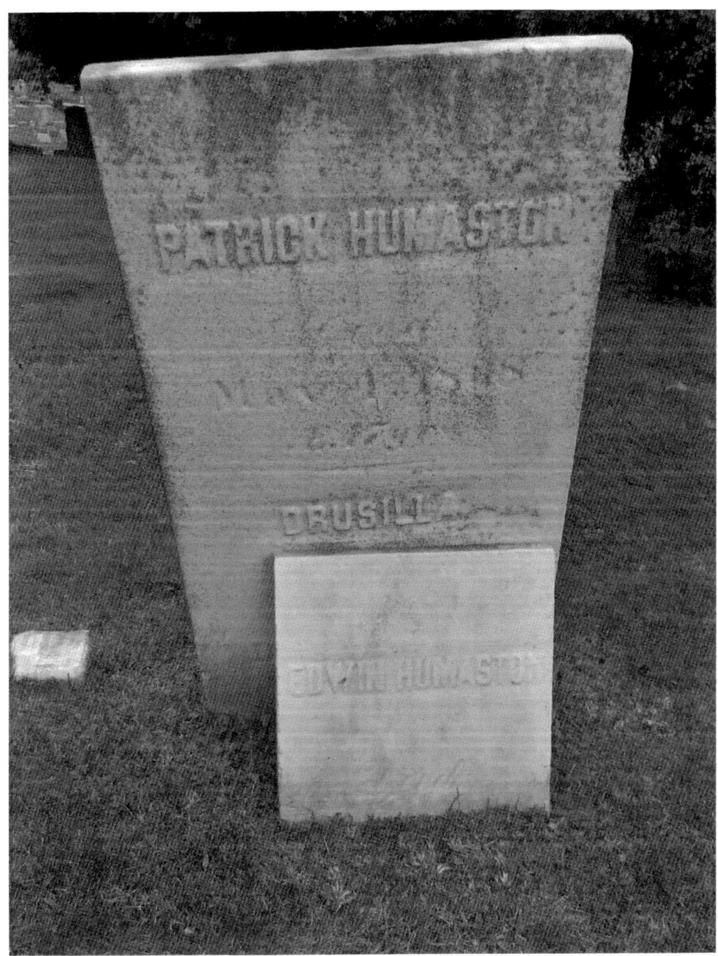

The headstone of Patrick and Drusilla Humaston at Woodvale Union Cemetery. *Author's collection.*

passed away at the tender age of twelve. Drusilla had been married to Hanna's fifteen-year-old brother, Patrick, and died in childbirth. Since there wasn't a township cemetery at that time, it was up to the area residents to select an appropriate burial site. This site was chosen on a small half-acre piece of land that had been part of the Eliza M. Fowles farm.

Drusilla Humaston's death was followed in 1837 by the death of Ammy and Hanna's two-year-old son, Ceylon E. Lovejoy. The next year saw two more interments: Ammy's infant niece, Triphenia Lovejoy, and Hanna's seventeen-year-old brother, Patrick Humaston Jr., who followed his wife,

Drusilla, to the grave just one and a half years after her untimely passing. Since there were now four interments in this plot, Ammy Lovejoy decided to purchase the burial ground from its current owner and properly designate it as a cemetery. So, on February 26, 1839, Ammy Lovejoy, along with neighbors Amos Gardner and Jeremiah Fuller, purchased the half-acre lot for fifty dollars from Eliza Fowles. The title transfer stated that it was to be used as a burying ground. The following year, Amos Gardner's thirty-year-old brother, Russel, was interred there.

In 1845, Solomon Lovejoy, one of the township's earliest pioneers, passed. It was at this time that Ammy took over the day-to-day operations of Lovejoy's Tavern on Turnpike Road. In 1849, Jeremiah Fuller's wife, Roxy Sprague, died. She left behind two small children, Phoebe and Morton. Jeremiah married two more times, first to Alma Fern and then to Lucy Humaston, Hanna's sister.

It should further be noted that these owners of the cemetery weren't just simple farmers. All three served as township officers in various positions from trustees to justices of the peace.

Two years after the death of Roxy Sprague Fuller, the community experienced loss again, this time in the passing of Amos Gardner's mother, Isabel, on Christmas Day 1851. Seven years later, Ammy lost another niece, Triphenia's twenty-one-year-old sister, Emily. In 1861, Amos Gardner's father, Paul, passed away, having outlived his wife, Isabel, by ten years. His death was followed, in 1865, by the death of Ammy Lovejoy's mother, Syrena. It was around this time that Amos Gardner, his parents both now deceased, decided to move with his wife to Wisconsin, where their daughter, Parmelia, had recently relocated with her husband, Lester Parsons.

The next two interments to take place in the burial ground occurred in 1867 and 1870. The first was Hanna Humaston Lovejoy, who died at the age of fifty-two. The following year, Ammy Lovejoy remarried, this time to a widow from Canada named Mary Ellen Glancey. The second interment was Jeremiah Fuller, who died at the age of sixty-six.

With Fuller now deceased and the Gardners residing in Wisconsin, Ammy Lovejoy decided to sell the burial ground to the trustees of Middleburgh Township with the expressed understanding that it would remain such. In the title transfer, two stipulations were made to protect the sanctity of this small cemetery. The first stated that the trustees were not to remove the bodies now at rest in that cemetery unless they had the consent of all interested parties. The other stipulation was that all parties owning lots in that cemetery were not to be disbarred from the grounds.

Be that as it were, no record of permission can be found regarding any allowance for the cemetery to be moved. It is uncertain when it occurred, likely sometime after the death of Ammy Lovejoy in 1891, but the graves of the fourteen people interred there were exhumed and relocated to Woodvale Union Cemetery on the northeast corner of Engle and Fowles Roads. Their gravestones now stand in section A.

Today, the site of the old Lovejoy/Gardner/Fuller Cemetery exists behind a property in Middleburg Heights along the west side of Big Creek Parkway, two houses north of Main Street and just before the high-tension power lines. The exact location, according to old maps and survey lines, rests behind the garage of that residence, just north of the bluff of Baldwin Creek, which cuts through the property. The site is on private property and is therefore not accessible to the public.

34
GATES CEMETERY

MOVED FROM A FIELD

Lat 41°22'12.166" N, long 81°49'04.325" W
41.370046, -81.817868
Status: Strictly Off Limits!

Stephen Gates Sr. was born in the early 1790s in Massachusetts. Later, he traveled with his wife, Elizabeth, and son to Ohio, seeking better opportunities. On October 10, 1851, he purchased a sizable piece of land in Middleburgh Township from John A. Granger, who at that time owned most of the area.

The following year, Elizabeth Gates passed away at the age of sixty-six and was buried in a small lot beside Bagley Road where it crossed the corner of the Gates property on a southeast course. On June 1, 1860, Lewis H. Gates, Stephen and Elizabeth's three-month-old grandson, passed. He, too, was buried in this lot. The following year, Stephen Gates joined them.

After this, the property passed to Stephen and Elizabeth's son, Stephen Gates Jr., who owned the land until 1881, when it was sold to Abram Fowles, a longtime neighbor. After the sale, the graves of those who were interred in the lot were exhumed and transferred to Woodvale Union Cemetery.

Other earlier interments on the site might have included neighbors Caleb Bentley and Philo Fowles, who died in the mid-1830s.

The only indication of this location ever having been used as a cemetery appears on the county map for 1858, which shows a rectangular section marked off from the rest of the surrounding land. Oddly, this site rests alone in a field. However, looking back at the 1852 map, one discovers that Bagley Road used to take a southeasterly turn much farther west than it did in later years. After the road was rerouted, the cemetery was left quite out of the way.

Today, the site of the former Gates Cemetery sits just to the north of the last house on the left at the north end of Grant Boulevard in Middleburg Heights. There is no trace of it ever being a cemetery, and the exact location is strictly off limits as it rests entirely on private property.

35

FITZWATER CEMETERY

BRECKSVILLE'S FORGOTTEN BURIAL GROUND

Lat 41°21'00.035" N, long 81°36'10.004" W
41.350010, -81.602779
Status: Strictly Off Limits!

The City of Brecksville currently owns and maintains five different cemeteries, only one of which—the Brecksville or "Highland Drive" Cemetery—is still open for burials. There are two, Riverview and Barr Road Cemeteries, that are of moderate size. On Brecksville Road, just north of the Squire Rich Museum, is the lone burial site of Revolutionary War veteran Benjamin Waite. Unknown to most people, though, is the Fitzwater Cemetery, located in an overgrown area near Riverview and Fitzwater Roads.

John Fitzwater Sr. was born on December 4, 1800, in Bucks County, Pennsylvania, not far from Philadelphia. Shortly after his birth, his family moved to Yates County, New York, where John's father, Joseph Reed Fitzwater, passed away in 1823. Due to imperfect land titles, the family was left with very little inheritance and had to make their way by working the land. It was in Yates County that John met and married his wife, Sabra Peckins, on December 26, 1822. Three years later, John and Sabra Fitzwater relocated with their children and John's mother, Catharine "Katie" Williams Fitzwater, to Elk, Warren County, Pennsylvania.

On January 10, 1836, John purchased a 103-acre tract, the whole of lot 101 in the northeast corner of Brecksville Township, from John and Aurillia Israel. That summer, he traveled by horseback to view his newly purchased land and returned with his mother, wife and children the following spring to live on it permanently. For the first two years, the Fitzwaters occupied a small hut that already existed on the property. Soon after, a frame structure was erected facing Riverview Road.

On January 5, 1848, Mary E. Fitzwater, the five-year-old daughter of John and Sabra, died. Two other children, Charles and Rachel, had previously passed away, but their deaths and burials had occurred in Pennsylvania. A new family burial plot needed to be selected. The site for this was chosen on a rise about two hundred feet west of the house.

Mary's death was followed by the passing of John's eighty-seven-year-old mother, Catharine Williams Fitzwater, on September 29, 1854. Her remains were laid to rest just a few feet away from Mary.

In 1873, John and Sabra Fitzwater decided to leave Brecksville to pursue sheep farming in White County, Tennessee. That year, they traveled south with their two youngest sons, William and John Jr., but the venture never came to fruition. On April 8, 1874, less than a year after departing Brecksville, Sabra Peckins Fitzwater passed away, just four months shy of her seventieth birthday. Her husband, John, followed her to the grave that August. Both were originally buried in White County, Tennessee, but were disinterred and their remains brought home by their sons John and William for reburial in the Fitzwater family plot.

Following the deaths of John and Sabra, the farm passed into the hands of their son William Henry Fitzwater, who would occupy it until his death in 1908. During his time there, he and his wife, Eliza Hunt Fitzwater, lost two children. The first was their two-year-old daughter, Alice Emma Fitzwater, who passed away on January 3, 1883. The second was their thirty-three-year-old son, Henry Earle Fitzwater, who died on May 14, 1896.

Henry's death was quite tragic. He had recently become engaged to a prominent young lady from Cleveland, and the two were to be wed soon. On that ill-fated day, he had been working in the fields under extremely hot conditions, and it is believed he suffered from a sudden disorientation of the brain, quite possibly heat stroke. That evening, after the rest of the family went to sleep, Henry went out to the barn and hanged himself from one of the rafters. His body wasn't discovered until sometime the following day. Both of William and Eliza's children were buried in the old family plot behind the house. Henry was the last one interred there.

Following the death of William Fitzwater in 1908, the farm was sold to his nephew, Myron E. Fitzwater. Myron continued to work the farm until the mid-1920s, when he began to subdivide the land and sell it off in individual

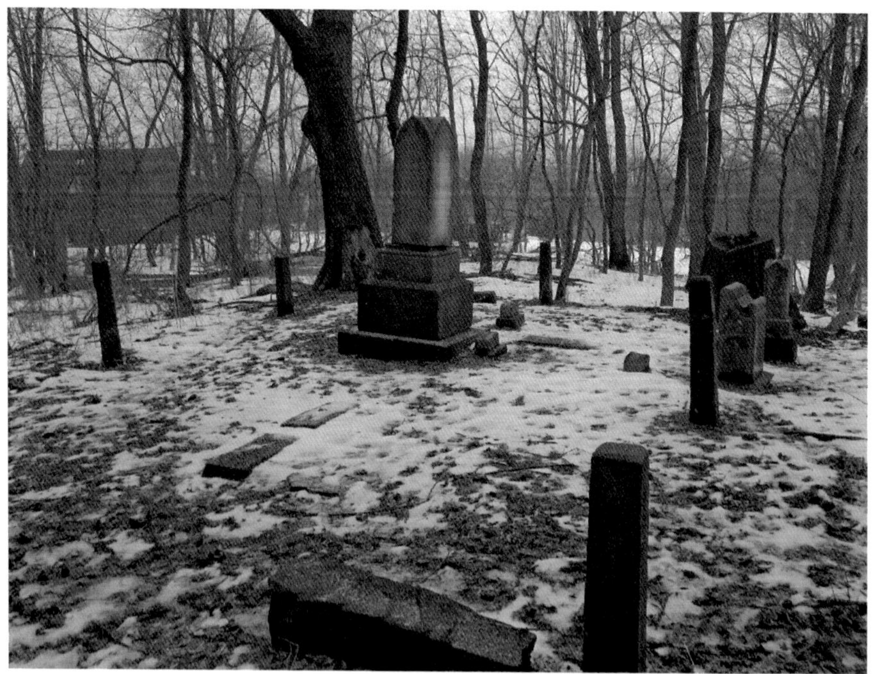

Snow covers the ground at the abandoned Fitzwater Cemetery in Brecksville. *Author's collection.*

lots. Thus, the Fitzwater farm passed out of the hands of that family, though the cemetery is still in their possession.

Today, the Fitzwater Cemetery exists in a small wooded area on a hill between Riverview Road and Park Place Drive, just north of Fitzwater Road in Brecksville. There is no longer an access road or right of way leading to the abandoned burial plot. Visiting this location is not recommended, as it is entirely surrounded by private property. It now stands at the top of a ten-foot easement in a sad state of disrepair, as it has been vandalized in the past. Perhaps in the future Brecksville will install an access way to this location, but until then, the site is strictly off limits.

Aside from the six burials mentioned, there are a few other scattered and broken grave markers around the site. There are also two concrete bases on the south end of the plot that have had their tombstones removed, and with them, all vital information about who is buried there. At one time, this cemetery was marked off by a set of stone posts and a chain that encompassed the grounds. Though the posts remain, the chain is long gone.

PART IV
NORTHWEST CEMETERIES

NORTHWEST CUYAHOGA COUNTY CEMETERIES WITH ORIGINAL TOWNSHIPS, CIRCA MID-1800S

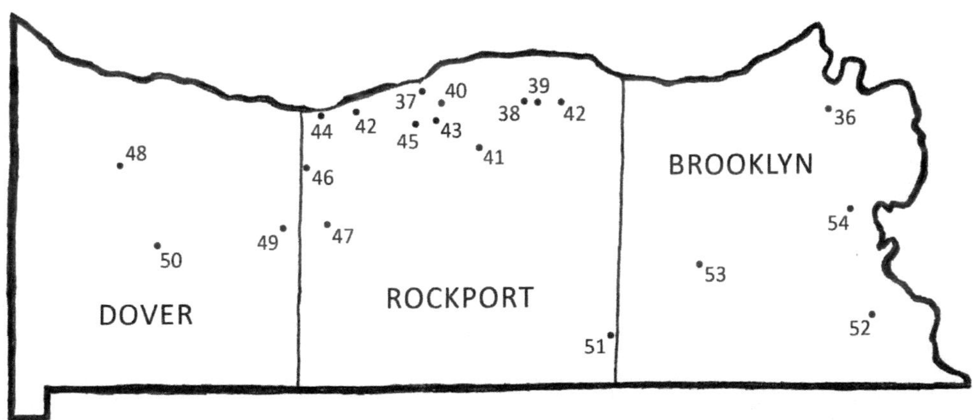

36. Ohio City Burial Ground
37. Chippewa Burial Ground
38. Wagar Cemetery
39. Kidney Cemetery
40. First Rockport Township Graveyard
41. Gleason/Edwards Cemetery
42. Two Rockport Estates
43. The Rockport Tumulus
44. McMahon/Hahn's Grove Cemetery
45. Wright Family Cemetery
46. Farr Cemetery
47. Lowell Family Burial Ground
48. Clemans Farm Cemetery
49. Sperry Family Plot
50. Dover Center Cemetery
51. John Mack Cemetery
52. Cutting Cemetery
53. Cleveland Pest House Burial Ground
54. Cleveland City Infirmary Graveyard

36

OHIO CITY BURIAL GROUND

FIRST ON THE WEST SIDE

Lat 41°29'04.364" N, long 81°42'07.627" W
41.484546, -81.702119
Status: Fully Accessible

Returning to Cleveland, we find the west side's counterpart of the Ontario Street Burial Ground. Both share a similar story, as well as a similar fate. The Ohio City Burial Ground was once located on what is now the intersection of Lorain Avenue and Gehring Street and was of a considerable size. It originally ran along the southern side of Lorain, from where it used to meet Abbey Avenue, east to the old intersection of Columbus Road.

This cemetery predates, by many years, the one located in Ohio City on Monroe Avenue, which was first established in January 1836. According to those who remembered its existence, it was originally a Native American burial ground that the first white settlers of Ohio City utilized to inter their dead.

The property on which it sat was first owned by the Lord family and was part of a 490-acre tract. It was sold on August 1, 1820, to Josiah Barber, Richard Lord's brother-in-law, and entered the possession of the Lord and Barber Realty Company shortly thereafter. In 1836, Barber and Lord dedicated the little triangle of land at the western end of the cemetery lot where Abbey Street met Lorain Street to Ohio City to be used for park purposes. Around this time, they had deeded the land for Monroe Street

Cemetery to the trustees of Brooklyn Township, a replacement for the old burial ground. Ohio City ordered the rest of the cemetery to be closed and burials there to cease.

The following year, the graves that could be located were moved from the cemetery to Monroe to make room for the ever-growing community of Ohio City. Barber and Lord subdivided the land the following spring and sold it off as individual lots. For a number of years after, children used the triangular lot at the western end of the old cemetery as a ballfield. Other lots that sat to the east had small houses built on them.

In 1851, Ohio City Volunteer Fire House No. 2, a one-story wooden structure, was built on the center of the small triangular lot. The land immediately adjacent was then being used as a pasture. Ironically, vandals burned down this firehouse on August 20, 1860. Less than a month later, a new two-story brick engine house was contracted. It was completed the following year with the designation Volunteer Engine House No. 10. On May 21, 1867, the Cleveland Fire Department was reorganized, and firefighters were no longer employed on a volunteer basis. The firehouse was recommissioned as Engine House No. 6.

By 1889, the firemen were outgrowing Engine House No. 6, which was in need of additions. While digging a cellar for one of these small additions, the firemen uncovered numerous human bones. Among the bones was a skull, which was kept in the engine house until it mysteriously disappeared in the summer of 1902. In an odd twist, stories were told for years regarding a haunting at this old firehouse. In one instance, the alarm bell gave out a single toll with no one there to pull the rope. From time to time, doors would open and close of their own accord.

In the late fall of 1898, a twenty-six-year veteran of the department, John Schwartz, reported being grabbed numerous times throughout the night. Thinking that it was a prank, he waited quietly, determined to catch the culprit. After a short time, the person appeared at the end of his bed. At this, Schwartz dove at the individual, but the apparition vanished through the ceiling. The fireman continued to witness the specter over the course of the next month or so, until his retirement that following February. He himself passed away quite suddenly just four months later.

Another story tells of a fireman named James McGreal being sent down into the cellar one evening to ignite the furnace. He returned quite abruptly and visibly shaken, claiming he heard a terrible groaning sound coming from across the room by an old box of wood shavings. When he went to

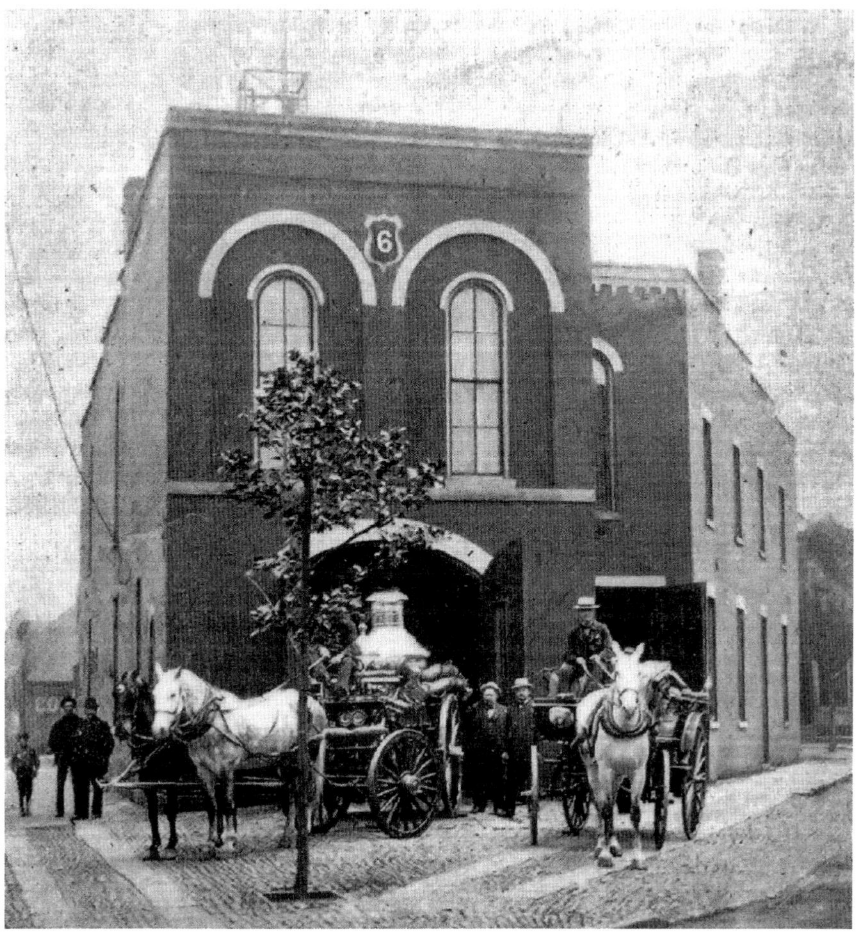

Engine House No. 6, which occupied the site of the Ohio City Burial Ground, circa 1898. *The Western Reserve Fire Museum and Education Center.*

investigate the source of the noise, a skeletal hand reached out and grabbed him. He never ventured into the cellar alone again.

Shortly after the turn of the century, Engine House No. 6 began to fall into disrepair and was torn down on August 11, 1904, to make way for a new engine house. At the time of its demise, it was the oldest fire station in the city. While digging a new cellar, workmen once again uncovered a number of bones, as well as a complete skeleton lying in what remained of a coffin. A doctor and a dentist examined the body and determined it belonged to a thirty-two-year-old woman who had been buried for many years. A lock of auburn hair still clung to her skull.

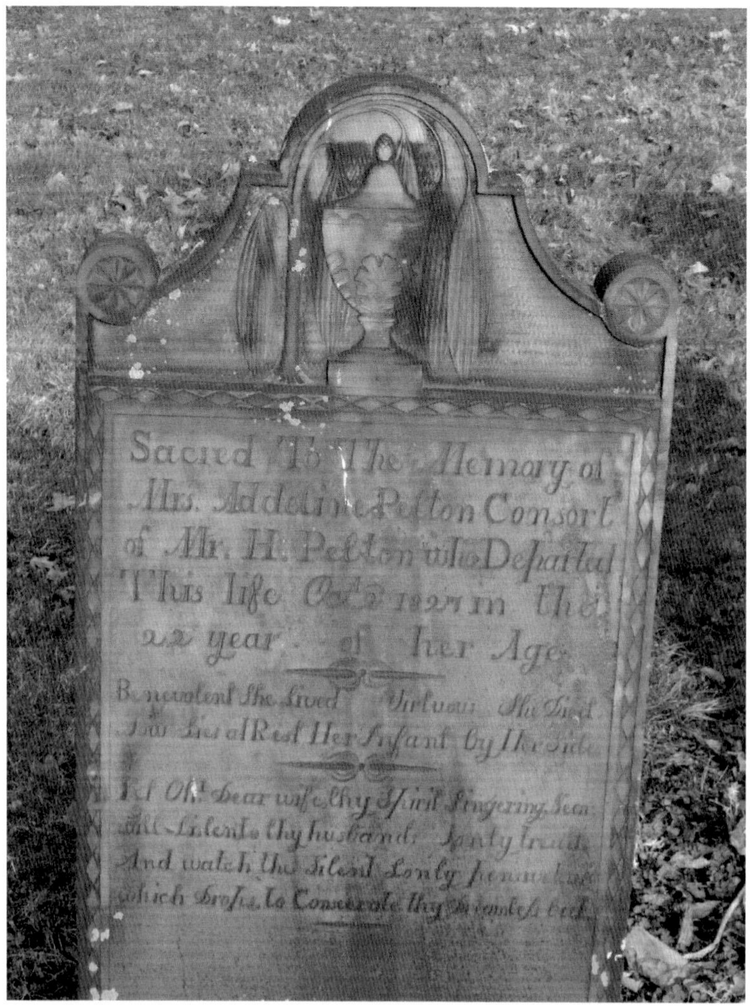

The headstone of Addeline Pelton, which was moved to Monroe Street Cemetery in 1836. *Author's collection.*

One area resident, a man well into his nineties, recalled the old burial ground on that lot. Furthermore, he and his wife had buried a daughter, Elizabeth, there in 1835. Seeing the remains that were uncovered made him wonder if her body had actually been removed to Monroe Street Cemetery. A local man who didn't want kids to start playing with the remains carried them away. He buried them that night in a secret location.

Previous mentions of Monroe Street Cemetery claim that burials took place there as early as 1818, but this is not the case, as the Monroe Street lot was in the middle of a farm field until the early 1830s, when the street was laid out. Tombstones that predate 1836 were moved from the old Ohio City Burial Ground. Among these is the headstone of twenty-two-year-old Addeline Tracey, the first wife of Halsey Pelton, who died while giving birth on October 2, 1827. Her sandstone grave marker, poetically engraved and adorned with fine images of an urn and willow, is located in section D and is in pristine condition.

Two other headstones, very similar in design, lie in that same section but have fallen to time and are lying flat on the ground a short distance to the east. These are the graves of Cornelius S. and Adam C. Taylor. The vital information from Cornelius's headstone is completely worn away, while Adam's marker tells us that he died on September 15, 1820, at the age of eighteen. Both stones are sinking into the earth and might be completely gone in just a few years.

All recollection of this first cemetery's existence has been lost for more than one hundred years. There are likely more human remains located on this site, but only further excavations will reveal that secret. Aside from being the intersection of Lorain Avenue and Gehring Street, the site is also occupied by the northeast corner of Market Plaza and the West 25th Street Rapid Station. Presently, the site is under consideration for redevelopment as a transit-oriented community. If the project comes to fruition, it will consist of retail stores, apartments and town houses within walking distance of the West Side Market, the shopping district along West 25th Street and the RTA Red Line. Construction workers may be in for a surprise.

37
CHIPPEWA BURIAL GROUND

INDIAN ISLAND/DEAD MAN'S ISLAND

Lat 41°29'15.522" N, long 81°50'05.895" W
41.487645, -81.834971
Status: Strictly Off Limits!

Located near the mouth of the Rocky River, this site originally consisted of three islands, with the largest one closest to the lake. It was here that, for many generations, members of the local Chippewa tribe buried their dead. One story from the early history of Cleveland tells of the death and burial of a man named Menompsy, which occurred around 1803. It is the first reported murder in Cleveland.

Menompsy had been a medicine man of the Chippewas and was called on to heal the wife of a man named Big Son, the brother of the Seneca chief Stigwanish. Sadly, Big Son's wife died while under Menompsy's care, and a disagreement over Menompsy's method of treatment ensued. That evening, after leaving Alexander Campbell's trading house on the east bank of the Cuyahoga River, the two men were walking up Union Lane, now West 10th Street. When they reached the top of the bluff, now the corner of West 10th and Superior Avenue, Big Son offered his hand to Menompsy as a gesture of peace. As Menompsy reached to accept his hand, Big Son drew a knife and stabbed Menompsy in the side. Within a few minutes, the medicine man was dead. Following his death, Menompsy's body was carried to the Chippewa burial ground on the large island at the mouth of the Rocky River and interred with his people.

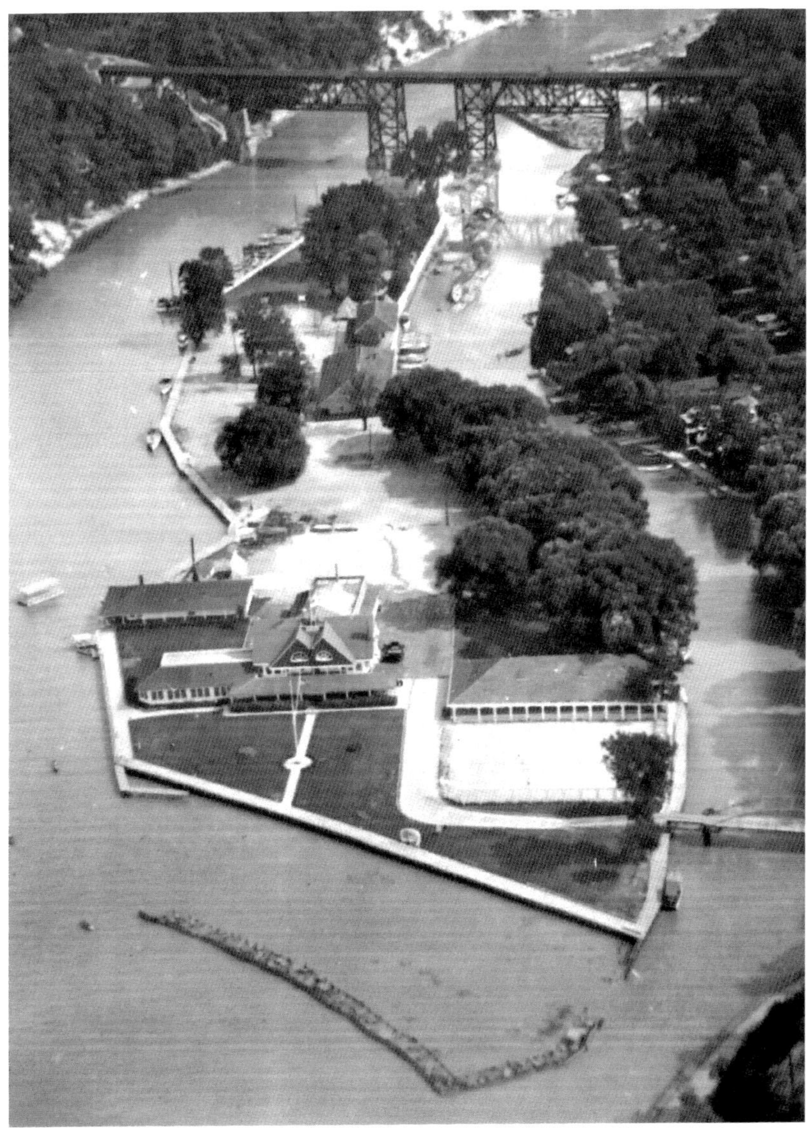

An aerial view of the island that contains the Chippewa Burial Ground. *Rocky River Historical Society.*

For many years after, the islands were uninhabited. Eventually, they fell under the ownership of James Ford Rhodes and Elias Simms, who developed the northwestern end of Lakewood. The small stretches of water between the three islands were filled in, and on February 2, 1907, the island was sold to the Lakewood Yacht Club. On June 15, 1913, the Lakewood Yacht Club sold the island to the Cleveland Yacht Club, and it has been in its possession ever since.

It has been rumored, but not verified, that Native American remains were uncovered during various construction projects on the island. The site of the burial ground now rests beneath the clubhouse and north parking lot of the Cleveland Yacht Club. The club is closed to nonmembers, but a glance down at the river from the north side of the Clifton Avenue Bridge will give a bird's-eye view of this ancient burial ground.

38

WAGAR CEMETERY

THE OLD SHORTCUT

Lat 41°29'06.162" N, long 81°47'52.378" W
41.485045, -81.797883
Status: Fully Accessible

Wagar Cemetery was established on a slight hill on the Mars Wagar farm (called Mapleside) in Lakewood between St. Charles and Belle on the south side of Detroit Avenue. Comprising about half an acre of land, the first burial there was Lucy Dwelle Wagar, Mars's sixty-year-old mother, in 1826. Two years later, he opened the cemetery to his neighbors. The final interment in this lot occurred in the early 1890s. For the better part of sixty-five years, this was the primary cemetery for the early residents of East Rockport, today's Lakewood.

According to Mars Edward Wagar, a grandson of the cemetery's original owner, no records were ever kept of burials, nor did the superintendent keep receipts. Digging the graves cost one dollar per burial and was a cash transaction. If one had the money, the grave was dug. If he or she didn't, there was no sale. Of course, everyone saw to it that there was enough money. Overall, no records were deemed necessary, and therefore, no books were kept.

As time and neglect began to take their toll on the Wagar Cemetery, Mars Wagar's descedants permitted advertising companies to use the land for billboard placement. Otherwise, it was used by local children as a shortcut going to and from school. With rumors circulating of the old burial ground

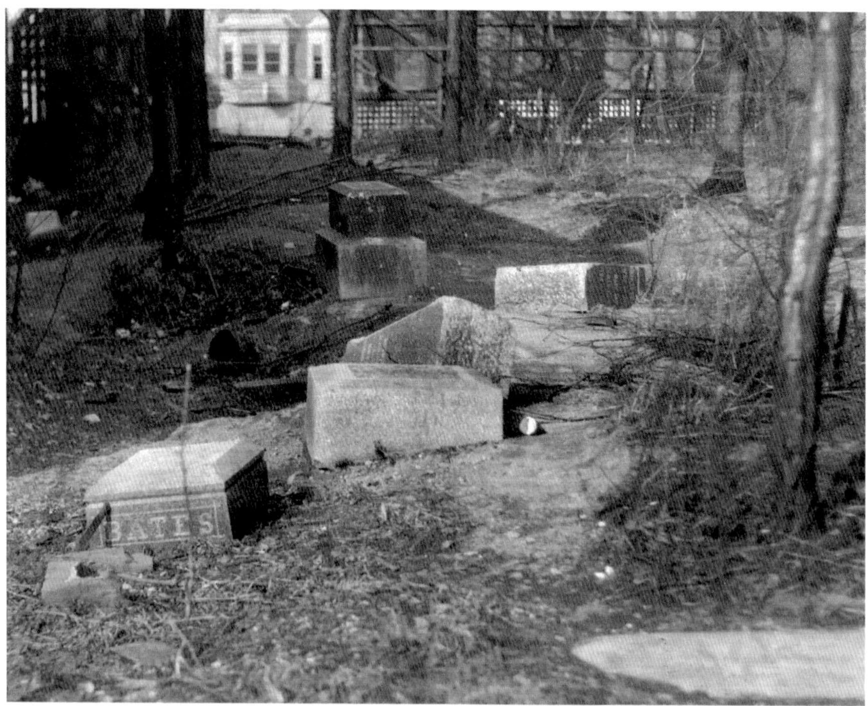

Vandalized and neglected headstones at Wagar Cemetery in Lakewood, circa 1930. *Cleveland State University. Michael Schwartz Library.*

being haunted, it became the scene of tombstone desecration and many childhood pranks. Furthermore, area children would sled down the front of the hill to Detroit Avenue during winter months.

In March 1951, Lakewood passed a city ordinance (number 4725) declaring Wagar Cemetery to be a public nuisance and prohibiting its further use. Furthermore, it requested all persons with family or friends buried in the cemetery to remove the remains or face having it done by the new owners of the property. Many bodies had already been removed by this point, as the cemetery was considered derelict. Lucy Wagar, the first burial, had been moved to Lake View Cemetery many years earlier.

Due to the lack of recordkeeping, it is unknown exactly how many people were buried at Wagar Cemetery. In August 1957, excavation began, and the remains of fifty-four people were exhumed. Among these were the remains of a little girl who was found to still have long golden braids and another girl who had been burned to death in a fire. These remains were placed in large black boxes and relocated to Lakewood Park

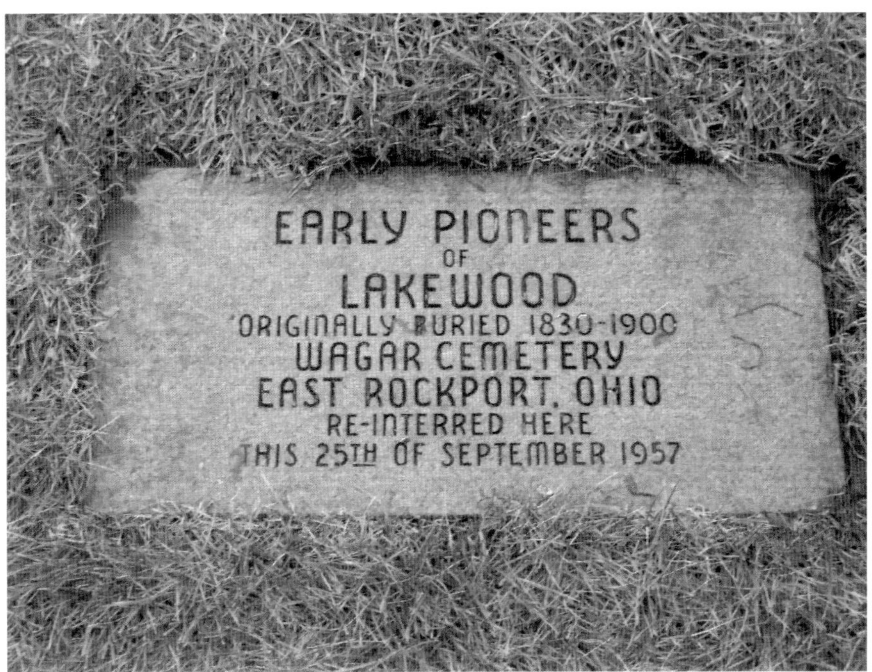

A single headstone marks the graves of those moved to Lakewood Park Cemetery from the Wagar and Kidney Cemeteries. *Author's collection.*

Cemetery in Rocky River, where, that October, they were buried in one mass grave in section 2. Since it was impossible to know who was buried in which plot, the tombstones having been vandalized over the years, the few tombstones that were found were moved to the city service garage and later to the herb garden behind the Lakewood Historical Society at Lakewood Park. Shortly after the removal of the graves, the rest of the site was bulldozed and paved over. Since there were very few headstones found, it is unknown how many sets of remains were left at the cemetery site and now sit beneath a parking lot and bagel shop.

39

KIDNEY CEMETERY

A SMALL FAMILY STRIP

Lat 41°29'05.359" N, long 81°47'51.453" W
41.484822, -81.797626
Status: Fully accessible

This small burial ground has the distinction of often being overlooked and considered a part of the old Wagar Cemetery. It was, in fact, a completely separate graveyard. In July 1828, Israel V. Kidney purchased the property just to the east of Mars Wagar's lands where Wagar had established a cemetery two years earlier. The Kidney Cemetery was set

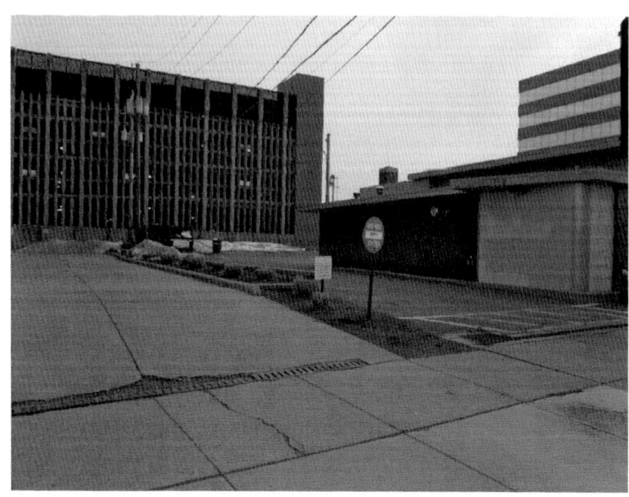

This driveway in Lakewood now occupies the exact site of the Kidney Cemetery. The parking lot and structure to the right mark the site of the Wagar Cemetery. *Author's collection.*

aside as a 16.5- by 162.0-foot lot that abutted the eastern edge of the Wagar Cemetery.

The exact number of people who were buried here is unknown, but the first interment was that of Sarah Ann "Sally" Kidney, the first wife of Timothy Seymour Brewster. She died on August 28, 1828, at the age of twenty-three. Another person known to have been buried there was Israel Kidney's wife, Catharine, who died on May 17, 1850, at the age of fifty-one.

As happened with the Wagar Cemetery, the Kidney Cemetery became neglected and vandalized. Those who were interred there were removed to Lakewood Park Cemetery in Rocky River. The last removal was twelve unknown sets of remains that were reinterred at Lakewood Park on September 25, 1957, in a mass grave in section 2, lot 301.

Today, the site of the old Kidney Cemetery is a driveway that runs between the parking lot of a bagel shop and an office building at 14601 Detroit Avenue in Lakewood.

40

FIRST ROCKPORT TOWNSHIP GRAVEYARD

THE CEMETERY AND THE HOTEL

Lat 41°29'01.327" N, long 81°49'41.959" W
41.483702, -81.828322
Status: Fully Accessible

Very little is known about the first burial ground in Rockport Township (which now covers Lakewood, Rocky River, Fairview Park and part of southwest Cleveland). For many years, this title was bestowed on the Wagar Cemetery on Detroit Avenue, but few were aware that an even older cemetery once existed at the northwestern end of Lakewood.

The first supposed burial in this graveyard, Nathan Alger, arrived with his family in Rockport Township in June 1812 and settled near what is now the neighborhood of Kamm's Corners, then known as the Alger Settlement. Alger lived for only another six months and died on January 21, 1813. It was assumed that Alger Cemetery in Cleveland was established upon his death, though evidence now points to the contrary. Accounts incorrectly refer to this first burial as being that of Henry Alger, and while Nathan did have a son by that name, Henry Alger died in 1862, long after the establishment of Alger Cemetery. It is now a controversial mystery whether Nathan Alger was originally buried in Alger Cemetery or at this forgotten site and later moved.

The second death to occur in the township was that of a deacon named Daniel Miner, who traveled from Homer, Courtland County, New York, to Rockport in 1809. Daniel Miner has the distinction of being the first person to be tried and convicted by the Cuyahoga County Courts. He was charged

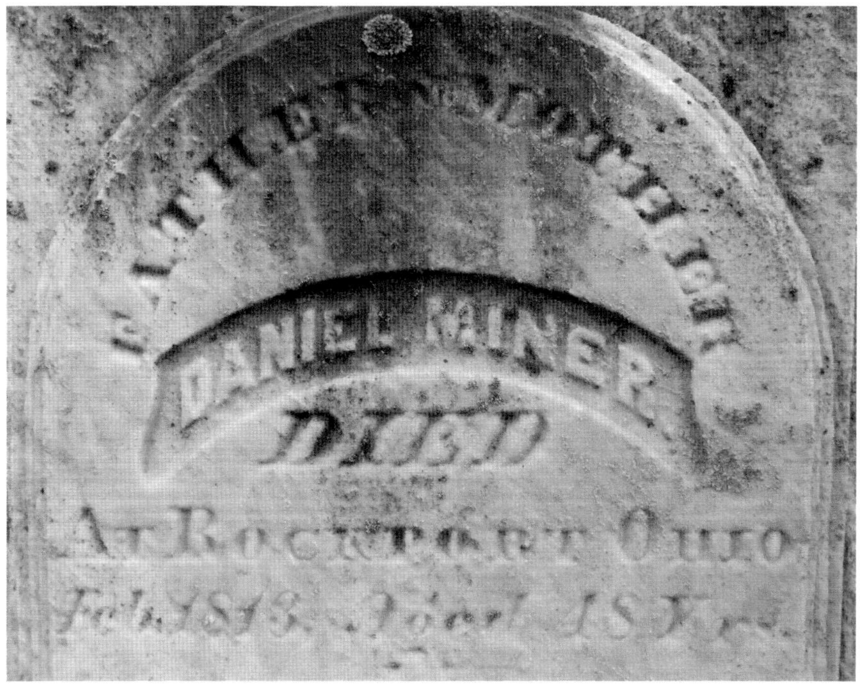

The epitaph of Deacon Daniel Miner at Woodlawn Cemetery in Norwalk. *Author's collection.*

in November 1810 with illegally selling whiskey and operating an unlicensed ferry across the Rocky River. He ultimately attained licenses for both of these and operated a ferry and tavern for the next few years. In 1812, Daniel Miner began construction on a mill along the Rocky River. He never saw its completion, dying in February 1813. It is also said that this cemetery was the burial site of many other early pioneers and a number of sailors who drowned off the point in 1812.

For many years, the early burial ground sat unnoticed and out of the way on what was known as Clifton Park. The graves were left undisturbed until a hotel and tavern were built on the site. The Cliff House was officially opened on Christmas Eve 1868 at the end of a dummy rail line called the Rocky River Railroad that traveled from Cleveland to the western end of Lakewood. During the 1870s, Joseph H. Murch purchased the hotel, and for a few years, it operated as the Murch House before being changed back to the Cliff House.

When this facility was constructed, the graves were removed to other cemeteries, most ending up at Alger Cemetery. Deacon Daniel Miner's

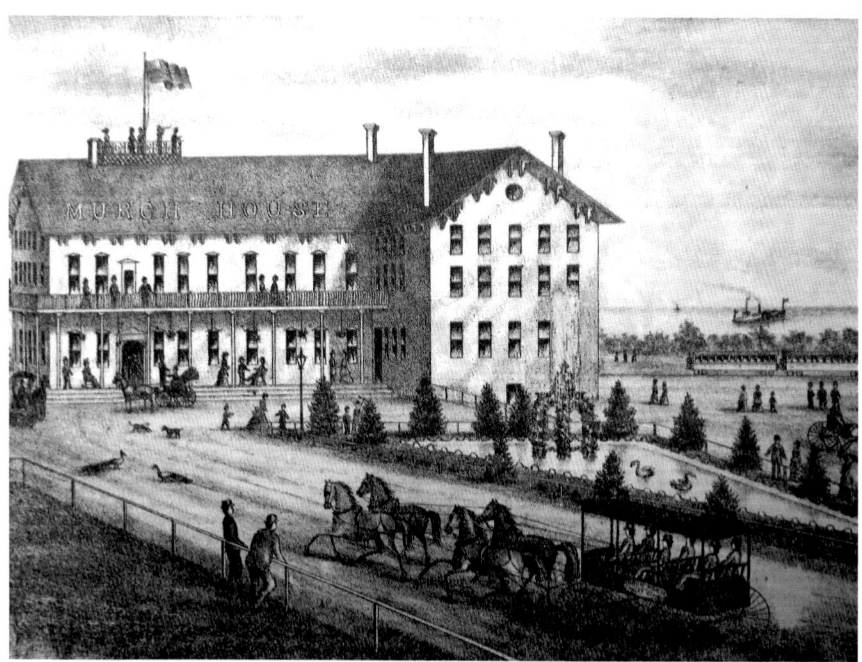

The Murch House, which was built on the site of the First Rockport Graveyard, in western Lakewood. *From D.J. Lake* Atlas of Cuyahoga County, *1874.*

remains were taken out to Woodlawn Cemetery in Norwalk, where he now takes his repose beside his wife, Avice, and son, Daniel Miner Jr.

The Cliff House operated until Halloween 1883, when it burned to the ground. An ember that had fallen from the stove in the downstairs kitchen caused the fire. Shortly after, the dummy rail line was taken over by the New York Central and St. Louis Railroad and now operates as the Norfolk Southern line.

The site of this former cemetery is now the intersection of Edanola Avenue and Riverside Drive in northwestern Lakewood.

41

GLEASON/EDWARDS CEMETERY

THE FAMILY PLOT ON THE HOGS-BACK ROAD

Lat 41°28'31.835" N, long 81°48'45.532" W
41.475510, -81.812648
Status: Strictly Off Limits!

On August 9, 2000, contractors working to replace a driveway in Lakewood made a startling discovery. It was here that they unearthed a headstone for a man named Jeremiah D. Gleason, who had died in 1868. The work continued, and five days later, a second headstone was uncovered. This one had been dedicated to the memory of Fanny Impett and her daughter, Betsey. Also located during this time was a sandstone statuette of a lamb. These artifacts were found resting in an area surrounded by a sunken stone and brick wall, consistent with what one might expect to find encompassing an early graveyard. A search was made of the area, but no human remains were located. Still, the question remained: who were these people and how did their stones end up at this site? A look into the lives of these early settlers yielded some answers.

Thomas Impett was born on January 26, 1800, in Preston, Kent, England. There, at Saint Mildred's Church, he married Fanny Chandler on July 15, 1826. Eight years later, a daughter, Betsey Manger Impett, was born to this union.

The Impett family immigrated to the United States during the spring of 1852 and settled in Rockport Township. Shortly after their arrival, Thomas Impett purchased a forty-acre farm and added another thirty-two acres in the following years.

On April 29, 1854, Thomas and Fanny's daughter, Betsey, married John Gibbs of Rockport. Sadly, it was a very brief marriage, as Betsey passed away on November 14 of that year at the age of twenty. Her mother, Fanny Chandler Impett, followed her on April 20, 1872.

Thomas Impett died a few years later and was buried at the Wagar Cemetery on Detroit Road in present-day Lakewood. Impett Park on Cleveland's west side is named for this family. Still, the existence of the Impett headstone unearthed beneath the driveway remains something of a mystery, as it was believed that Fanny and Betsey were also buried at Wagar Cemetery. It is possible that they were originally buried on this site, as it was rather close to the Impett farm, and were later relocated to Wagar Cemetery. Sometimes stones just get left behind.

The existence of the Gleason stone made more sense.

Jeremiah D. Gleason was born on September 23, 1793, in Durham, Middlesex, Connecticut, to Jonas Gleason and Abigail Danforth. Seven years later, the Gleason family relocated to Greene County, New York, where Jeremiah found a bride in Catherine Dedrick. He traveled to Rockport Township in 1831 with his wife and six children. On November 16 of that year, he purchased a 130-acre farm along what was known as the Hogs-Back Road. Five years after arriving, a son named Gilroy (or Villeroy) was born. The only evidence of this child exists in the 1840 census, and a name is given in the Gleason family records. Gilroy died during the mid-1840s, and a small family cemetery was established on the Gleason farm at his passing.

The next to be interred there was Jeremiah and Catherine's daughter Emeline, who died in 1848. Just two years earlier, she had become Mrs. George Buskirk. Her death was followed three years later by that of her sister Elizabeth Nancy Gleason. Elizabeth had been married to Roswell Randall Edwards just three years prior. Their mother followed them in 1855 and their father, Jeremiah, on November 21, 1868.

Four other burials known to have taken place there were those of Jeremiah's son Wallace Gleason's children. Eugene, Dora, Julia and Edward Gleason died between 1867 and 1882. Their mother, Julia Alice Page Gleason, was the last person to be interred there. She died on October 9, 1898.

This small family cemetery was moved on January 2, 1908. Present at the exhumation was seven-year-old Edwin Thomas Mullaly, a grandson of Wallace Gleason, who watched with an aunt as the graves were removed. Many years later, he recounted the memory of this to his daughter, Alice Mullaly Fowler, who in turn shared the information with the Lakewood Historical Society.

Nine sets of remains were relocated that day to Evergreen Cemetery in Westlake and were reinterred in section H, lot 3. This lot had recently been purchased by Wallace Gleason, who died the following October and was laid to rest beside his family. Not relocated from the original family plot was Gilroy Gleason. His remains were never located and likely still remain on that site. No record of the Impett family being relocated exists.

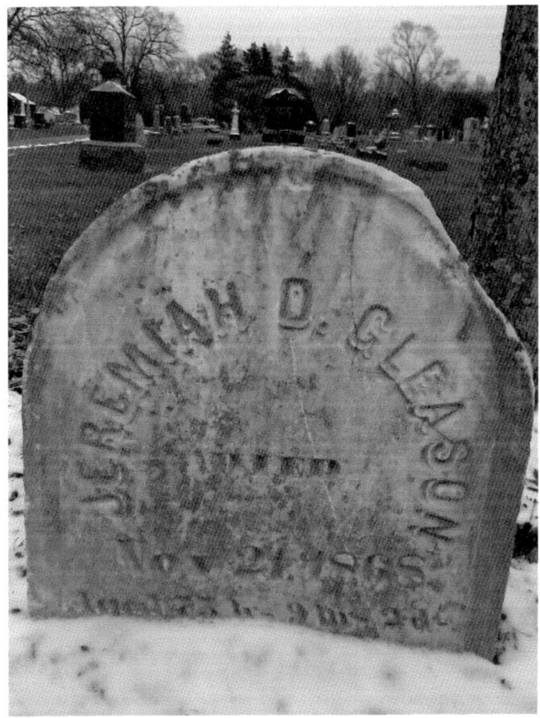

Unearthed beneath a driveway on Hillard Boulevard in Lakewood, the headstone of Jeremiah D. Gleason now marks his burial site at Evergreen Cemetery in Westlake. *Author's collection.*

When the stones were discovered in 2000, the Impett stone was sent to the Lakewood Historical Society and now rests among the gravestones that were once located at the Wagar Cemetery. The stone for Jeremiah D. Gleason was placed at his grave site in Evergreen Cemetery. Also set at this time was a small marker dedicated to those members of the Gleason and Edwards families who are now interred there.

Today, the site of the old Gleason Edwards Cemetery rests on the south side of Hilliard Boulevard under the third driveway east of Eldred Avenue. While it rests entirely on private property, it can easily be viewed from the sidewalk.

42
TWO ROCKPORT ESTATES

A GOVERNOR'S GRAVE

Lat 41°29'01.575" N, long 81°51'07.952" W
41.483771, -81.852209
Status: Partially Accessible

A stately home called Evergreen Place was originally located on what is now the southwest corner of Wagar Road and Avalon Drive in Rocky River. It was the residence of Ohio's twenty-first governor, Ruben Hazen Wood. The house had been built during the early 1830s by local carpenter, and later prominent Cleveland banker, James Pannell.

Ruben Wood was born in Vermont in 1793 but was educated in Canada. He was pressed into the British military to serve in the War of 1812 but successfully escaped back into the United States, where he was held briefly under suspicion of espionage. In 1818, Wood came to Cleveland and was admitted to the Ohio bar. Seven years later, he was elected to the Ohio Senate and served on the Ohio Supreme Court. In 1850, he was elected governor of Ohio and held that position until 1853. He'd even put in his bid as the Democratic candidate for the 1852 presidential election but lost the nod by one vote.

Governor Ruben Hazen Wood died at Evergreen Place on October 1, 1864, and was buried on the grounds of that house beside his mother, Lucretia Lockwood, who had died in 1839. Just over a year later, both

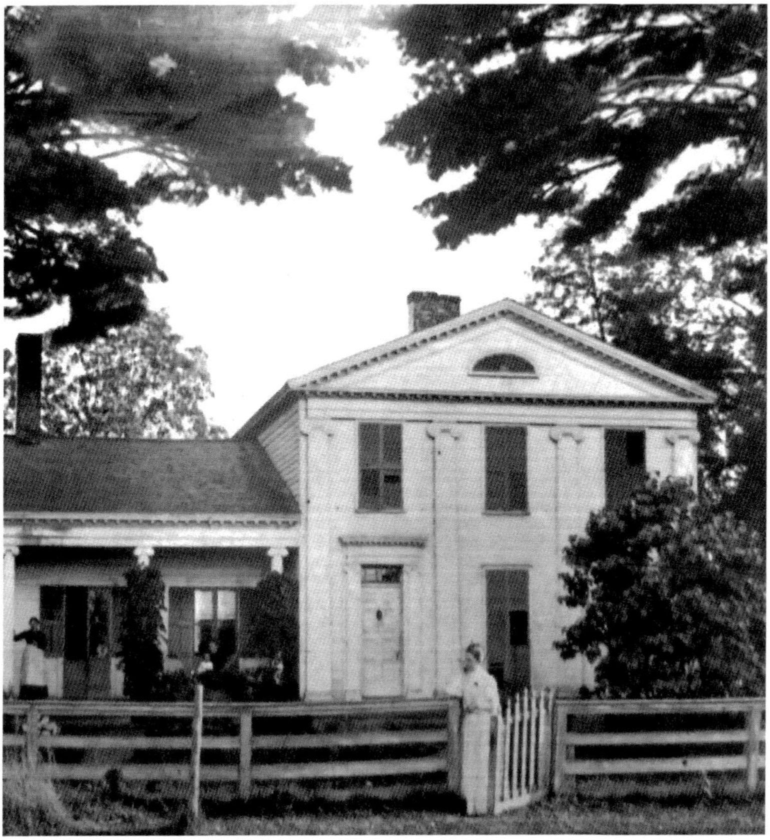

Above: Evergreen Place, the Governor Ruben Hazen Wood Residence, circa 1860s. *Rocky River Historical Society*.

Right: Governor Ruben Hazen Wood. *Rocky River Historical Society*.

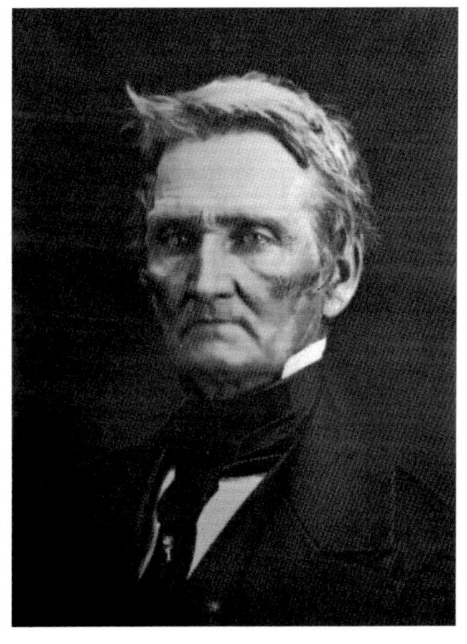

Governor Wood's and his mother's remains were exhumed and reburied at Woodland Cemetery in Cleveland in section 21, lot 44.

Many years later, a couple of tombstones were discovered at Evergreen Place being utilized as paving stones in a walkway. These were likely the late governor's original headstone and a piece of his mother's stone. A new headstone had been placed at his burial site at Woodland Cemetery when his remains were moved there. His mother's original tombstone sits beside this, though it is completely illegible and damaged, with a significant piece missing.

THE NATURALIST

Lat 41°29'06.266" N, long 81°47'25.930" W
41.485074, -81.790536
Status: Fully Accessible

Professor Jared Potter Kirtland was born in Wallingford, Connecticut, on November 10, 1793, to Turhand Kirtland and Mary Potter. Turhand was named land agent to the Connecticut Land Company and brought surveyors and settlers to Cleveland during its first few years of existence.

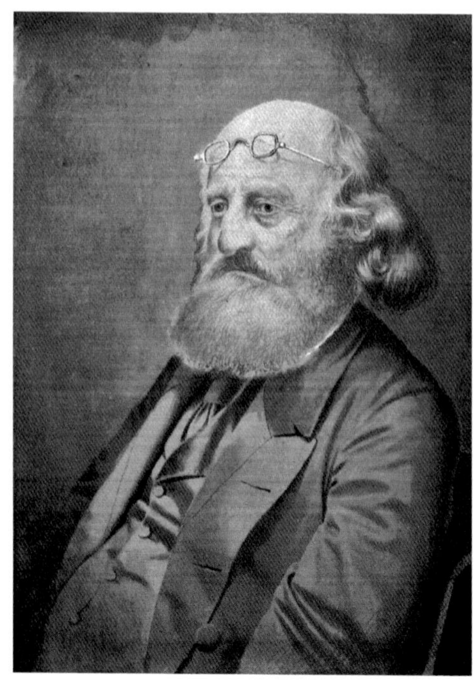

Professor Jared Potter Kirtland. *Lakewood Historical Society.*

In 1811, Jared Kirtland received an education at Yale University and, within a few years, married his wife, Caroline Atwater. Sadly, Caroline passed away in 1823 at the age of twenty-seven. Within a few years, Professor Kirtland removed with his children from Connecticut to Ohio, where he first stayed in Mahoning County to live with the rest of his family, who had settled there many years earlier.

Two years after the passing of his first wife, Professor Kirtland married again, this time to Hannah F. Toucey. The couple moved to Cleveland in 1837 and, two years later, settled in East Rockport, now Lakewood. It was there that Professor Kirtland built his country estate of Whippoorwill Villa, which comprised 150 acres that stretched from Madison Avenue to Lake Erie. On this estate, he grew a great variety of exotic flowers and fruits. It is also where he discovered a new species of warbler, which he appropriately named the Kirtland warbler (*Setophaga kirtlandii*).

Throughout his life, Professor Jared Potter Kirtland had many accomplishments, both in the political arena and in the field of natural science. He served in the Ohio House of Representatives and was also a probate judge. He published many papers on the natural world and was a physician, naturalist and a co-founder of what would become University Hospital, as well as the Cleveland Museum of Natural History.

Professor Kirtland died at his home on December 10, 1877, and was interred in a small family cemetery that sat behind the fine house in Lakewood. He was laid to rest alongside his second wife, Hannah; his two

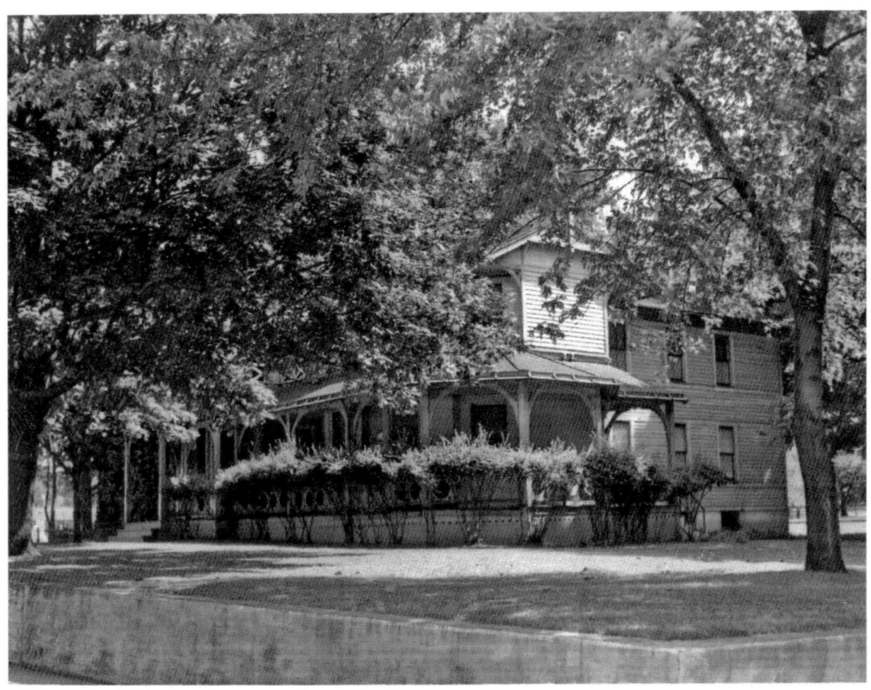

Whippoorwill Villa, the residence of Professor Kirtland, circa 1950. *Lakewood Historical Society*.

grandsons, Frank K. Pease and Charles Pease Jr.; Charles Jr.'s wife, Hester; and their daughter Mary. His remains sat undisturbed in this location for five years until his son-in-law, Charles Pease Sr., had the remains of everyone exhumed and moved to Lake View Cemetery. This occurred on April 25, 1883, with the reburial taking place the next day.

Whippoorwill Villa stood near the corner of Madison Avenue and Bunts Road well into the twentieth century. It was razed to make way for a grocery store that occupied that site into the early twenty-first century. The exact location of the old Kirtland Family Cemetery is on the southwest corner of a property that now is occupied by the Giant Eagle GetGo Gas Station. The driveway that enters this gas station from Park Haven Row crosses the former burial ground.

43

THE ROCKPORT TUMULUS

A MUCH-DEBATED BURIAL MOUND

Lat 41°28'56.482" N, long 81°49'47.722" W
41.482356, -81.829923
Status: Fully Accessible

Not to be confused with the First Rockport Graveyard, which sat very close to this location, the Rockport Tumulus became the subject of debate and controversy when it was first excavated more than 150 years ago. This tumulus, or burial mound, covered an area approximately sixteen feet by sixteen feet square and rose about two to three feet higher than the surrounding grounds. It was first observed in the 1820s by early settlers in the area, who found it contained human bones and decided against disturbing it. Some of the bodies it held were buried quite shallow, as many of these bones were found sticking out of the earth. The first impressions were that it was a Native American burial site, but those thoughts soon faded with the discovery of what it actually contained.

The site of this mound, as described by the previously mentioned Professor Jared Potter Kirtland, sat on the bluffs above the east bank of the Rocky River, about 150 feet east of the old Plank Road Bridge over the river. It was positioned at the head of a gully that once cut from the high ground to the bottomlands, near the bridge that existed in the 1860s. At one time, this gully was the only way to gain access to the bluffs above the river and surrounding country. By the late 1860s, the gully had been partially obliterated by the construction of Riverview Road, which once ran along that area of the ridge.

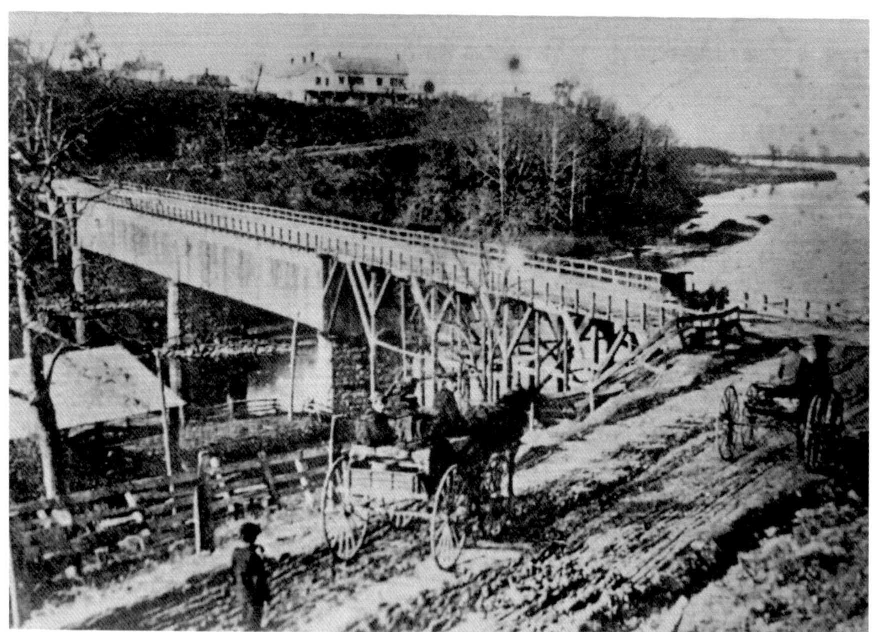

Old Detroit Road Bridge over the Rocky River. Photo taken near the site of the Rockport Tumulus, circa 1860. *Rocky River Historical Society.*

This was long before the Detroit Avenue Bridge approach in Lakewood was constructed. However, using present-day Detroit Avenue as a frame of reference, this road would have run south along the ridge to the present Riverview Road. The northerly section became Sloane Avenue.

In 1850, a man named Worden attempted to plow down the tumulus but found the furrows consisted primarily of human bones. Other artifacts also turned up, including metallic buttons and rusty pieces of iron, which his young sons collected. It was slowly becoming evident that this was not a Native American burial mound, as the indigenous inhabitants of northern Ohio did not possess such items. Worden decided to reinter the bones and leave the site alone.

In 1861, another farmer by the name of Eaton plowed into it again. He, too, turned up many bones and decided to gather them together. He presented the relics, which included many human skulls, to Professor Kirtland. After thoroughly examining the find, Professor Kirtland was convinced that these were the remains of males between their early adulthood and middle age. Furthermore, they were all Anglo-Saxon. A colleague of his, who was at that time considered to be the foremost "craniologists" in the country, confirmed this.

The following year, Professor Kirtland visited the site with a friend of his, a man named Kirkpatrick, and decided to excavate the center of the tumulus to the bottom, some two or three feet down. They discovered that the bottom tier of skeletons had never been disturbed. One set of remains, they believed, was Native American, as it was found with artifacts that would have belonged to such a person. They concluded that these remains had been buried in haste, much as one would expect to find on a battlefield. In all, the tumulus contained around seventy bodies.

Though their locations were quite close to one another, there is no way this was part of the First Rockport Township Graveyard. To begin with, that cemetery was still in existence when Professor Kirtland conducted his excavation with Mr. Kirkpatrick on the tumulus in 1862. The First Rockport Graveyard wasn't removed until around 1867 or 1868. Furthermore, it contained the headstones of early area pioneers. Professor Kirtland described no such markers at the tumulus. He also gives its location as being 150 feet east of the old Plank Road Bridge. The First Rockport Graveyard sat almost 700 feet northeast of this location.

So, if it wasn't the Rockport Graveyard and it wasn't a Native American burial mound, what was it and who was buried there? Professor Kirtland put forth a theory. In the early 1760s, two maritime disasters occurred on Lake Erie. One, it is well documented, happened within just a couple of miles of the tumulus. The exact location of the other has never accurately been determined. The events surrounding these disasters are as follows.

In 1763, the British had recently gained victory over France in the French and Indian War. Not satisfied with the outcome, an Ottawa chief named Pontiac began to lead raids with his people against the British-occupied forts in the western territories along the southern shore of Lake Erie and western Pennsylvania. Many forts were destroyed and their garrisons slaughtered. History came to call these events Pontiac's Rebellion, which lasted from 1763 to 1766.

In the fall of 1763, Major John Wilkins of the Royal Americans Sixtieth Foot was ordered to bring a detachment to Fort Detroit and put an end to the rebellion. He set out with six hundred British army regulars and reached Lake Erie at Fort Niagara in mid-autumn. They attempted to cross the lake in a fleet of bateaux (flat-bottomed barges used for transporting troops) but never reached their destination. At eleven o'clock on the night of November 11, the expedition was driven ashore by a violent storm. The results were catastrophic. Between eighteen and twenty of their boats were lost, along with their provisions, ammunition and artillery. In all, seventy men and three officers—including their surgeon, Dr. Williams of the Eightieth British Regulars—had drowned. Following the wreck, the expedition was abandoned and the survivors returned east.

The second disaster occurred almost a year later. This happened when Colonel John Bradstreet was likewise sent on an expedition to Fort Detroit with fifty bateaux, 350 British Regulars, 1,000 Provincials and 800 Native Americans. They successfully reached Detroit but, on their return to Fort Niagara, met with an unfortunate fate. On the night of October 19, while somewhere between present-day Sandusky and Lorian, a sudden storm blew up, and the fleet made an attempt to press through it. Ultimately, they decided to find a safe landing and thought they had finally discovered one but were unaware of a treacherous sand bar looming just off shore. The boats became either stranded on this bar and fell to the fury of the lake or were dashed to pieces against the rocky cliffs. In all, Bradstreet lost twenty-five bateaux along with most of his supplies and artillery. It is unknown exactly how many men were lost. Today, the site of this disaster is a park in Rocky River called Bradstreet's Landing.

In regard to the Wilkins disaster, it has often been debated on which side of Lake Erie this event occurred. The only location referred to in any documents is a place called Point-Aux-Pins or Pine Point. There is one location on the Canadian shore that is called that, but the name was not yet applied at the time of the disaster. Dispatches sent to Fort Detroit from the wreck site took eleven days to arrive. Had they been in Canada, a trek like that through friendly country would have taken only two days at best. Should the courier have had to move at night through hostile country, such as Ohio, eleven days is more realistic. Some surmise that Point-Aux-Pins might refer to Tisdale's Point, which was the name given to the northwest edge of Lakewood, later, as previously mentioned, called Clifton Park. Many have argued the site of Wilkins's disaster to be near Rondeau, Ontario, just across the lake from Cleveland. It seems likely to some that Wilkins would have taken a northerly course across the lake, the shortest distance between Fort Niagara and Fort Detroit, yet we know that Bradstreet had taken a southerly course for his return. It was also noted in a journal that Wilkins had ordered the bateaux to keep well out from shore. How far out is not said.

That relics from at least one of these disasters have been found in great abundance between Bradstreet's Landing and northwest Lakewood is doubtless. These artifacts include muskets, bayonets, cannonballs, coins and swords. Of particular interest is an old surgeon's amputating knife that was found buried beneath a few inches of soil. There was no surgeon listed among Bradstreet's troops. Could this have belonged to Dr. Williams of the Eightieth British Regulars?

In truth, with the site of the Rockport Tumulus now totally obliterated by urban development, there's no way of excavating further to make any accurate conclusion about who was buried there. Professor Kirtland was certain that these were the victims of one of these disasters. With Wilkins losing seventy-three men and the site containing approximately that number, he points to the likelihood of these being Wilkins's men. Still, he contends that the number who perished under Bradstreet's command is unknown, though he believes that the number lost must have been great, as it became the subject of legislative action.

The site of the Rockport Tumulus, by best geo-mapping and estimation, is now occupied by the northwest corner of Sloane and Detroit Avenues, just east of the Rocky River Bridge, in Lakewood. No trace of its existence remains.

44

McMAHON/HAHN'S GROVE CEMETERY

A SUMMER RESORT

Lat 41°28'56.359" N, long 81°52'12.029" W
41.482322, -81.870008
Status: Fully Accessible

Many years ago, Cleveland-area residents enjoyed a summer weekend at the resort in western Rocky River known as Hahn's Grove. Little did they know, a small burial ground was located on the property.

This piece of land was originally part of a 69.7-acre tract owned by Michael and Julia Benedict McMahon, who arrived in 1833 from Connecticut. On the land, they established a small cemetery to inter the deceased members of their family. In October 1861, Michael McMahon died from consumption and was buried there beside his children and grandchildren. Among them was his fourteen-year-old daughter, Susanna, who had died in 1851 from dysentery. Ten years later, his widow sold the property to Charles Hahn.

To make extra money, Hahn opened the northern section of his land as the beachfront resort Hahn's Grove. Almost immediately, he forbid any further burials to take place in the old cemetery. This included Julia McMahon, who died on August 4, 1898, just two months shy of her ninety-eighth birthday.

The cemetery was located on a slight rise close to the lake and is now the site of the Beach House, a high-rise condominium just west of Bradstreet's Landing on Lake Road in Rocky River. On October 27, 1914, the remains of Michael and Susanna were exhumed and reinterred at Alger Cemetery in Cleveland with those of Julia. No trace of the cemetery exists today.

45

WRIGHT FAMILY CEMETERY

THE POSTMASTER'S BURIAL SITE

Lat 41°28'51.136" N, long 81°50'06.630" W
41.480871, -81.835175
Status: Partially Accessible

Captain Rufus Wright earned a small piece of fame one September day in 1813, when he received a dispatch in Sandusky from Acting Lieutenant Dulaney Forrest. The dispatch had been sent from Commodore Oliver Hazard Perry and was to be delivered to General William Henry Harrison some eighty miles away. It contained the famous letter bringing news of victory following the Battle of Lake Erie: "We have met the enemy and they are ours." As legend has it, Captain Wright couriered this dispatch through many miles of dense woodlands and hostile country until he successfully handed it off to the waiting general. He had made the journey in one day, an incredible feat.

The good captain was born in 1771 in Stillwater, New York, to Job Wright and Sarah Ursula Carpenter. By the onset of the War of 1812, he had already been married for a number of years to his wife, Hepsibath St. John, and was the father of many children. Following the war, Captain Rufus Wright returned to New York, where he convinced his family that prosperous lands lay to the west. Thus, the Wrights traveled to Ohio in 1816 and settled in what was then called Granger Village in Rockport Township, now the northeasterly part of Rocky River.

Within the first year, Captain Wright built Wright's Tavern on the western bluff overlooking the river. In early 1819, the first township election was held in the tavern. A view of the tavern can be seen in the image in the section on the Rockport Tumulus. As fine a tavern as it might have been, there still existed the problem of accessibility. No regular ferry service had operated on that river since the death of Deacon Daniel Miner in February 1813. Thus, Rufus Wright decided that he would restore the ferry service to bring people safely across the river. In 1821, he resigned himself to the notion that a permanent crossing needed to be established and constructed the first bridge to span the Rocky River. Its location was roughly in the area beneath the present-day Detroit Avenue Bridge.

In 1834, Captain Wright took on the position of postmaster of Granger Village, an occupation he held for quite a few years. He was succeeded by three of his sons, Abraham Ephraim Wright, who held this position until his death in 1848; Philip Wright, until his death in 1853; and Frederick. It was Frederick who became the most prosperous.

At the age of twenty-three, Frederick acquired a 204-acre tract of land, though it was slowly whittled down to 43 acres in later years. A house was erected along the North Ridge Road (later called Detroit Road) between what is now Prospect and Wright Avenues in Rocky River. It stood into the early twentieth century. Frederick primarily tended fruit trees on the land.

Sitting a short distance to the southeast of the house was the little cemetery where the Wrights interred their family members. Buried there were Captain Rufus Wright (1771–1856), Hepsibath St. John Wright (1778–1855), Philip Wright (1803–53) and Abraham Ephraim Wright (1813–48). Also interred on this ground were various members of the Wagar family.

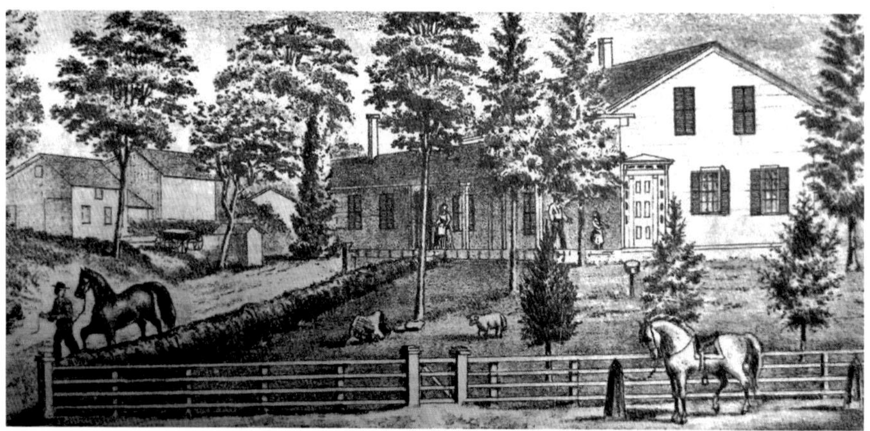

Frederick Wright Residence. The Wright Family Cemetery sat just to the east, behind the barns (left). *From D.J. Lake* Atlas of Cuyahoga County, *1874.*

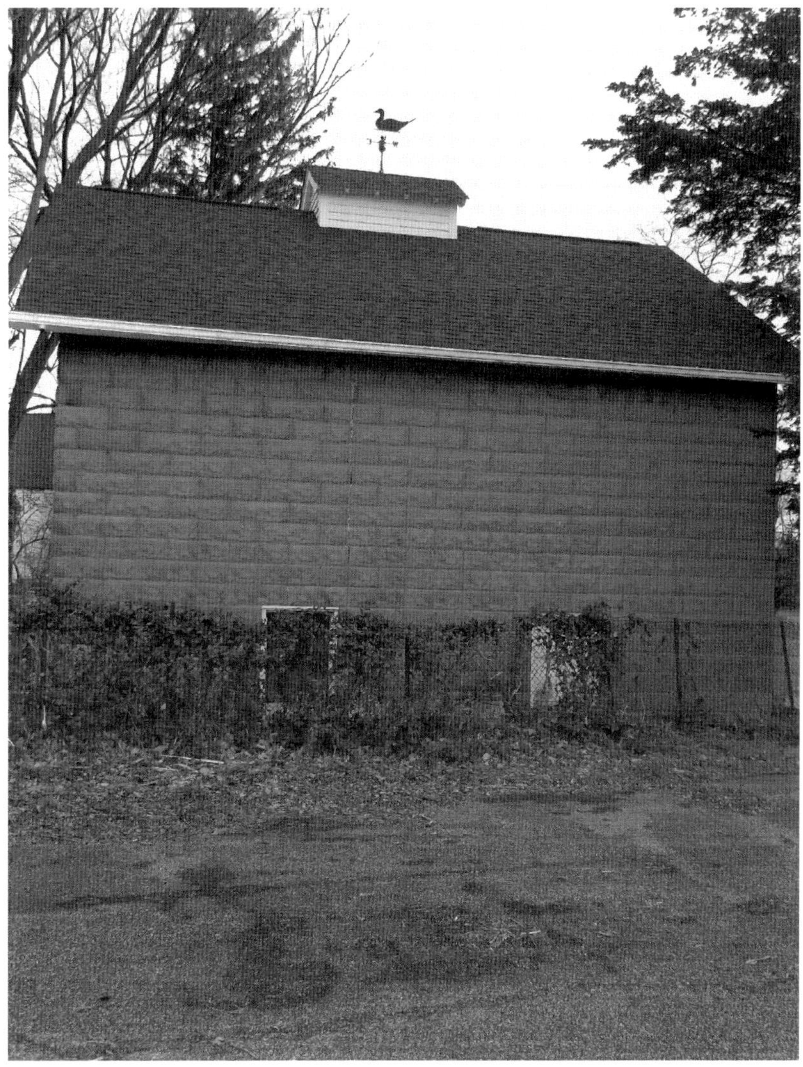

A parking lot, just to the north of this old milking barn, now occupies the site of the Wright Family Cemetery. *Author's collection.*

Oddly, Frederick and his wife, Dorothy, were not buried there. They were interred in Fairview Park at the Old Rockport Cemetery. Following Frederick Wright's death in October 1882, the Wright farm was divided, and the land that contained the old family burial ground was granted to Mary Elizabeth Arnold, Frederick and Dorothy's daughter, who owned it for a number of years.

According to Jack Nickels of the Rocky River Historical Society, the cemetery was mostly located about four feet north of an old milking barn that Arnold built on the property. Just before the outbreak of World War II, he and his scouting troop had done a search of this burial ground. There, they rediscovered the many tombstones of the Wright and Wagar families.

During the late 1950s, the land was again subdivided and the City of Rocky River purchased the parcel that contained the little cemetery. Ironically, the land was used for the construction of the new Rocky River Post Office, which opened in 1959 at 1647 Wright Avenue. When the back parking lot was being installed, the headstones were again discovered and removed. Their fate is unknown. Some years later, a grocery store was built on the lot just to the east of this site and further stones were uncovered. These ended up in the possession of the city but were lost over time.

Today, the site of the old Wright Family Cemetery is covered by the southeast corner of the parking lot of the former Rocky River Post Office, which was relocated in 1977. The old milking barn still stands just to the south of this lot and is a good point of reference when trying to pinpoint the cemetery's exact location. Just to the east of the old milking barn sits a wooded area in the backyard of the house next door. The ground is covered with a telltale patch of creeping myrtle. More headstones might still exist in this area but are concealed by the myrtle or have sunk. The parking lot of the old post office is easily accessible, though it is now being used as a business, and loitering for long periods of time is not encouraged. The balance of the cemetery that rests just to the east of the old milking barn is on private property and is therefore strictly off limits.

46

FARR CEMETERY

LOST IN THE ROUGH

Lat 41°28'15.478" N, long 81°52'25.136" W
41.470966, -81.873649
Status: Fully Accessible

Located in Rocky River on the south side of Detroit Road on the Westlake border sits what was once the Farr Cemetery. This land was originally part of a forty-nine-acre tract purchased by Aurelius Farr from Samuel and Sophronia Crocker on October 16, 1820, for $200. The Farr family had come to Rockport Township from Pennsylvania the previous year. It was on this farm, which eventually grew to one hundred acres, that they flourished and prospered.

The Farr Cemetery was established on the northwest corner of the lot and extended fairly deep into the property, being approximately half an acre in size. Since most of the old burial ground has been relocated, it's difficult to know exactly who was buried there. There are only two large tombstones that remain, as well as the fragments of two more, and those are located in the back of the old cemetery. At the front of the property, you can clearly ascertain where a walkway had once bisected the burial ground.

The first stone still located at the back of the property is a white marker that stands as a memorial to the members of the Taylor family. Henry Taylor was born in Lenox, Berkshire County, Massachusetts, on September 28, 1779. He married Elizabeth Barnes in September 1810 and, a few years later, traveled west to Ohio with his new bride and younger sister

Abigail. Elizabeth Barnes Taylor died in 1860 and was buried at the site. Her husband joined her two years later. Also interred there is Henry and Elizabeth's five-year-old daughter, Jane (1827–32), and their son Dexter R. Taylor (1815–51). Dexter was married to Jemima C. Lent on January 1, 1845. The couple had only one child, a daughter named Elizabeth. Sadly, Elizabeth lived for only five months and passed away on December 1, 1846. Her mother, Jemima Lent Taylor, followed her to the grave less than four months later.

The other stone that still stands on this site is a large, dark granite monument that only bears the name "Dean." The rest of the stone has been damaged, and there are no epitaphs or dates to tell us truly who is buried there. It is known, though, that Henry Taylor's sister Abigail married Chester Dean in 1818. Chester was recently widowed, his first wife, Lucy Smith Dean, having passed away the previous year. Chester Dean was a prominent early farmer who had arrived in Rockport in 1811 and was a brother-in-law of Datus Kelley, for whom Kelley's Island is named. His marriage to Lucy Smith was the first in Rockport Township, taking place on January 7, 1814. Chester Dean died on November 2, 1838, at the age of fifty-three. Abigail Taylor Dean continued to work the Dean farm until her death on August 9, 1881, at the age of eighty-six.

The third trace of a cemetery appears in the form of a small, rounded piece of limestone that rests on the ground beside its base. The only engravings that can be discerned from it are "rd P." The fourth and final trace is a carved piece of stone that doesn't match any of the other three on the site. This piece bears no engravings.

On November 4, 1913, the Farr property was sold to the Ridge View Land Company, which had plans to develop the site into a country club. Reserved from this sale, for one year's time, was the half-acre burial ground. In the months that followed, the descendants of those buried there made the necessary arrangements and had their loved ones' remains and monuments relocated to other cemeteries. Most of the Farr family ended up at Butternut Ridge Cemetery in North Olmsted, while the majority of the cemetery's occupants were reinterred at Evergreen Cemetery in Westlake. An exception to this was Julia Benedict McMahon, who was moved to Alger Cemetery in Cleveland and laid to rest with her husband and daughter in one grave.

In 1926, the Westwood Country Club took over the property and commenced building the golf course, regardless of what was left behind. The northwest corner of the cemetery lot is now the site of St. Peregrine's Chapel, where countless others might still be buried in now unmarked

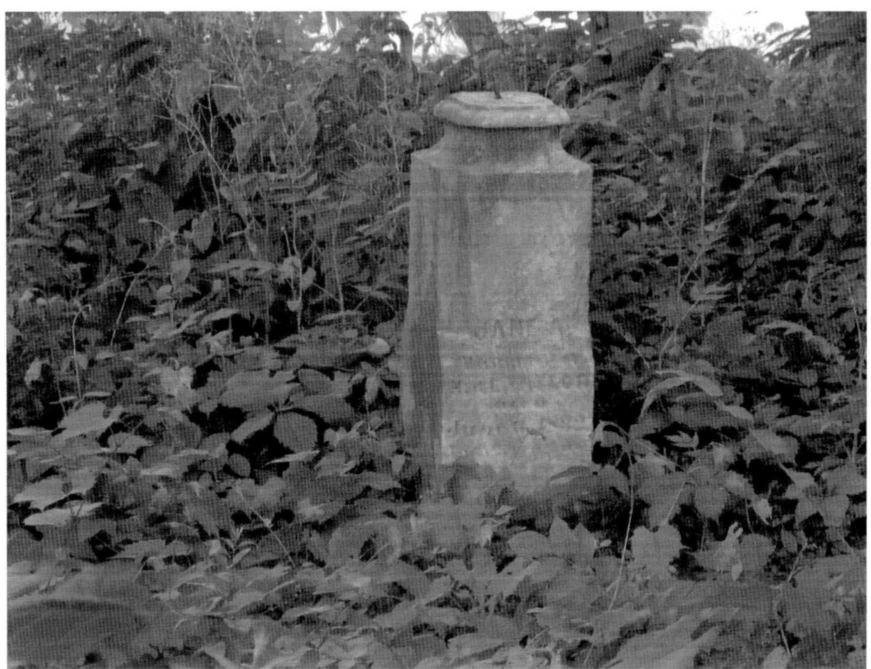

The Taylor family headstone at Farr Cemetery on the western border of Rocky River. *Author's collection.*

graves. The golf course still encompasses the back of the old lot, and it is here among the creeping myrtle and weeds, just beyond the parking lot for St. Peregrine's, that the tombstones for the Dean and Taylor families can be found.

On April 7, 1851, an obituary for Dexter R. Taylor appeared in the *Plain Dealer* and read:

> *He departed this life with a comfortable assurance of a blessed immortality beyond the grave. He has left a numerous circle of friends to mourn his loss. During his sickness his sufferings were great, but we trust he rests from his sorrows.*

47
LOWELL FAMILY BURIAL GROUND

THOMPSON CEMETERY

Lat 41°27'28.569" N, long 81°51'57.920" W
41.457936, -81.866089
Status: Partially Accessible

The Lowell Family Cemetery was located on what is now the southwest corner of Spencer and Center Ridge Roads in Rocky River. The Lowells settled on this land in the early 1830s, when it was originally owned by Gideon Granger of Ontario County, New York. In 1837, the land, which comprised fifty-one acres, was titled to Sidney Lowell and his wife, Mary Ann Whitney. This cemetery was approximately one hundred feet by one hundred feet.

Likely buried there are Sidney Lowell's parents, Timothy Lowell (September 28, 1780, to September 2, 1835) and Phebe Lowell, who died between 1840 and 1850. Also likely interred there are his uncle, John F. Lowell (February 7, 1797, to March 20, 1836), and two young daughters who died between 1840 and 1850. Also believed to have been buried there was William Cunningham, the first white settler to inhabit Kelley's Island, for whom that island was originally named.

Definitely buried there are two settlers from Middlesex County, Connecticut, named Enos Brainard (July 29, 1781, to February 2, 1848) and his wife, Sally (March 5, 1779, to July 1, 1844). According to *The History of Cuyahoga County*, compiled by Crisfield Johnson in 1879, Enos Brainard came to Cleveland in 1814 with Isaac Hinckley, Asa Brainard, Elijah Young,

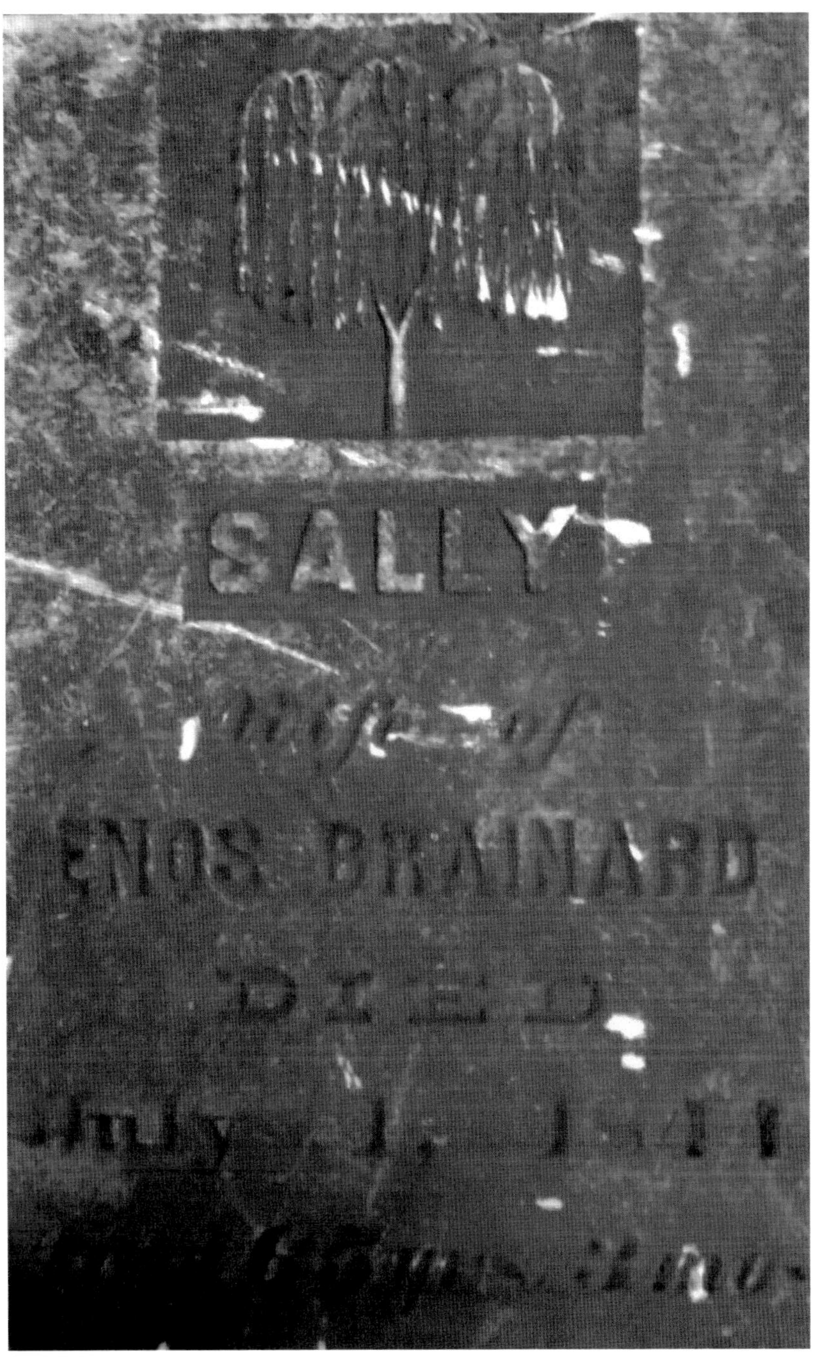

The headstone of Sally Brianard, now in the possession of the Rocky River Historical Society. *Author's collection.*

Steven Brainard and Warren Brainard. They all set out for Ohio on the same day in a wagon train that consisted of six wagons drawn by ten horses and six oxen. All journeyed together until they reached Euclid, forty days after leaving Chatham, Connecticut. Enos Brainard was a cooper by trade. He first lived in Cleveland, then Brooklyn and Strongsville, before finally settling in Rockport in 1835.

When excavation was underway for the development of Nantucket Row in 1994, a contractor unearthed a tombstone behind the unit that was closest to the intersection. It was about four feet by eighteen inches in size, white limestone in nature and was found lying flat beneath three inches of soil. The stone read:

Sally
Wife of
Enos Brainard
Died
July 1, 1844
Aged 65 yrs. 3 mos.

Previously listed genealogical records give her date of death as July 2, but these were recorded many years after the fact, and the headstone is likely to be more accurate. With her husband passing away only four years later, it is certain that he was buried beside her. Had the excavation extended a few more feet, it's very probable that his stone would have been unearthed as well. Not knowing what else to do with Sally Brainard's headstone, it was handed over to the the Rocky River Historical Society.

No other intact stones have been located on the grounds, though partial fragments of limestone and sandstone litter a nearby landscaped hillside.

When Sidney and Mary Ann Lowell sold the property to Mercy Carter Abell (a daughter of early Cleveland settlers Lorenzo and Rebekah Carter) in 1853, the cemetery was mentioned on the title transfer as "reserving from there ¼ acre in the northeast corner, now used as a burying ground."

This cemetery has also been known as the Thompson Cemetery, as the Thompson Gardening Company owned the property throughout the 1920s. Today, much of the site sits in a backyard on Nantucket Row and is strictly off limits, though the sidewalk on the southwest corner of Spencer and Center Ridge also cuts over a section of this burial ground and is fully accessible.

48

CLEMANS FARM CEMETERY

ABANDONED IN A FIELD AND FORGOTTEN

Lat 41°28'03.619" N, long 81°55'52.032" W
41.467672, -81.931120
Status: Fully Accessible

This small cemetery was one of the earliest to exist in Dover Township (now Bay Village and Westlake) in western Cuyahoga County, the first being Lakeside Cemetery on Lake Road in Bay Village. The property was part of a one-thousand-acre tract owned by Jedediah Crocker and cleared by his son, Noah. According to tombstone transcriptions that were recorded in 1931 by the Daughters of the American Revolution, the first burial on this land was Private Jasher Taylor, who served with Lieutenant Samuel Bartlett's Company in the American Revolution following the same alarm on April 18, 1775, that had called John Crosier to action. Private Taylor passed away at a nearby farm on August 6, 1827.

The second burial was that of Noah Crocker, who died just two months later at the age of forty-four. Over time, other members of the Crocker family would be buried there, but their graves were removed to Evergreen Cemetery in Westlake in 1878. Unfortunately, Noah's headstone was left behind, and many years passed before it was reunited with its owner. Other burials at this site include Joseph Bidwell of Rockport, Lucy Kingsley Phinney, Priscilla Gardner Sawyer and members of the O'Brien family. Also buried there was Elizabeth "Sibbel" Taylor, a sister of the previously mentioned Dexter R. Taylor and granddaughter of Jasher Taylor.

In its earliest years, when heading west, Detroit Road took a gradual northerly course and stopped at Cahoon Road. The road was routed in this manner to avoid a house that once sat on the brow of the ridge. After turning south on Cahoon Road and returning to the ridge, Detroit Road started up again and continued west. Some years later, the house that graced the brow of the ridge was leveled, and the course of Detroit Road was straightened. The little cemetery was now left in a field some distance from the main road and was soon after abandoned.

The burial ground property eventually fell under the ownership of the Eli Clemans family, and in the fall of 1931, the headstones and graves that could still be located were removed to Evergreen Cemetery. Lucy Fiore, a great-great-granddaughter of Lucy Kingsley Phinney, was a witness. She recalled that her father and an uncle had carried out the work. Furthermore, she was able to help pinpoint the exact location of the former cemetery site, something that has eluded historians for many years now. Her best recollections place it between an old cow barn and the former home of her grandfather, Alberto C. Phinney, on Cahoon Road. Much of this was

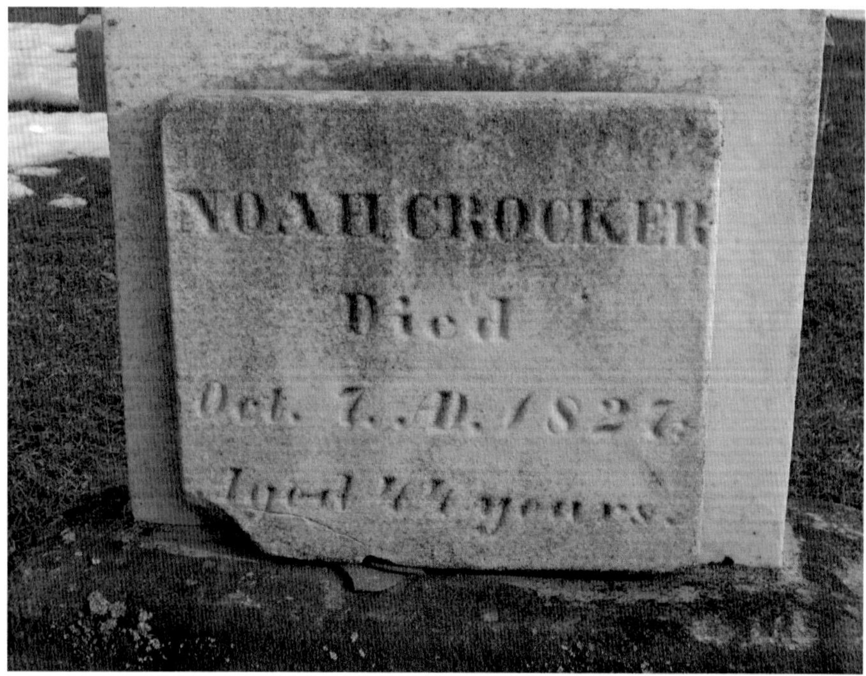

Noah Crocker's headstone, recovered after many years, now stands with those of his family members at Evergreen Cemetery in Westlake. *Author's collection.*

corroborated by her sister, Janet Wood, who recalled that the site ended up becoming the backyard of the Harder house. When Interstate 90 was routed through the area in the 1970s, the houses along Cahoon Road were demolished, and the road itself was rerouted to the west.

Today, the site of the Clemans Farm Cemetery rests near the southeast corner of the former Five Seasons Family Sports Club in Westlake. It now exists as a grassy patch between the parking lot and the embankment of the rerouted Cahoon Road.

49
SPERRY FAMILY PLOT

HORWEDEL/SPERRY CEMETERY

Lat 41°27'23.058" N, long 81°52'45.648" W
41.456405, -81.879347
Status: Fully Accessible

When Evergreen Cemetery was established in Dover Township in 1828, residents finally had a prime location to bury their dead. Prior to this, many buried their dead on family farms. This was the case for the Sperry family.

Amos Sperry had come to Dover Township from New Haven, Connecticut, around 1810 and operated a tavern on Center Ridge Road just east of Clague Road. On February 26, 1818, the Sperry family suffered two tragic losses. Amos's first wife, Dorcas Peck, and their daughter Rachel both passed away. Their cause of death was not listed, but both were interred in the plot on the family farm.

Shortly after, Amos married Hannah Ingraham, the widow of Junia Beach. Her first husband had died from the flu a year earlier in Elyria, and Hannah relocated to Dover Township with her children shortly after.

This cemetery is known in some records as the Horwedel/Sperry Cemetery because it once sat on the border of lands owned by the Sperry family and Edward Lawrence Horwedel. Horwedel's wife, Alice Mitchell, was the great-great-granddaughter of Amos Sperry, and it was through her that the land came into that family's possession.

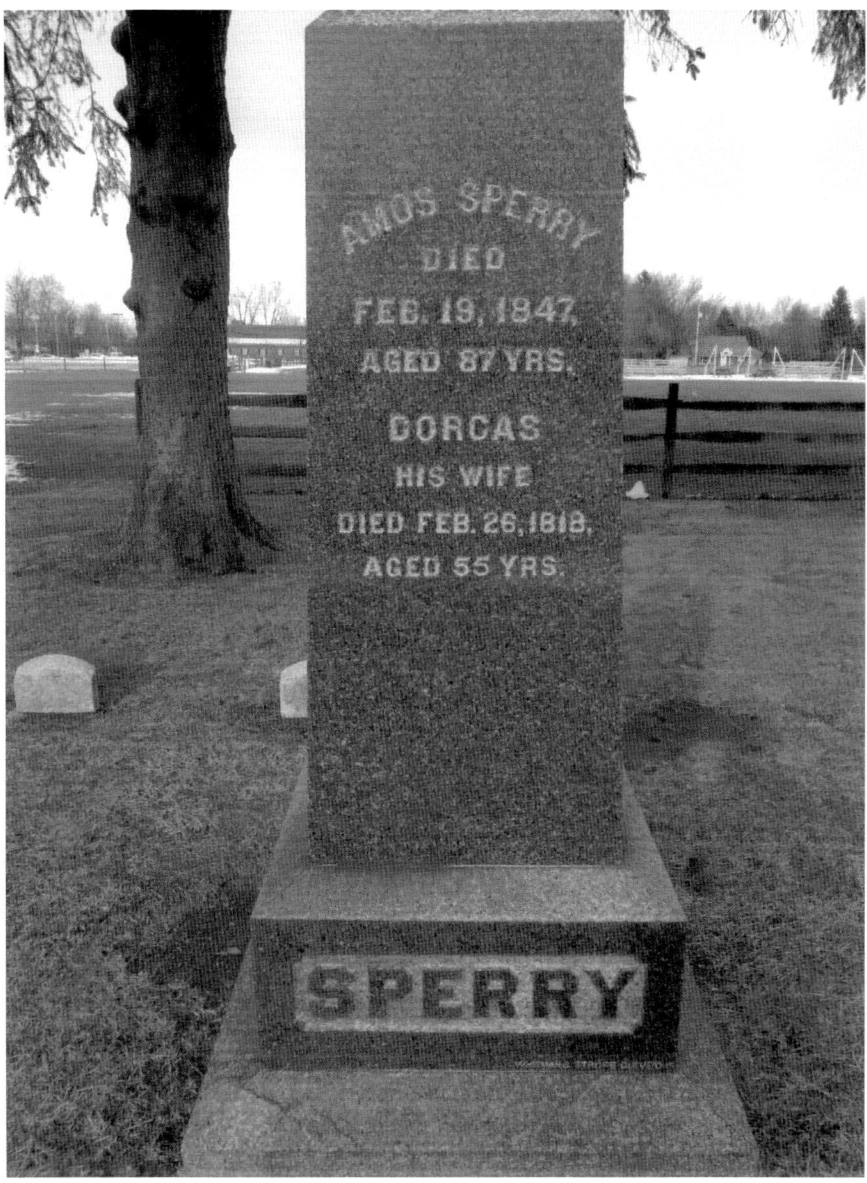

The Sperry family monument at Evergreen Cemetery. *Author's collection.*

Further records vaguely state that the cemetery was located near the intersection of Clague and Center Ridge Roads, though a better estimate places it on the east bank of Sperry Creek on the south side of Center Ridge Road in Westlake.

It should be noted that Amos Sperry was never interred in this family plot. He died in 1847 and was buried at Evergreen Cemetery about three miles west of his family farm. Eventually, this cemetery was cleared, and any graves that could be located were moved to Evergreen. Also relocated to the new lot at Evergreen were Junia Beach and his ten-month-old son, Lyman. Records do not indicate if they were ever buried at the Sperry Family Plot.

It is not known exactly when the Sperry family plot was moved, but the monument that now rests at the family's grave site was constructed by the firm Whitman and Strope of Cleveland. This was a fairly short-lived enterprise, lasting only from 1884 to 1888. It is likely that these graves were moved during this era.

It should also be noted that Rachel Sperry, Amos and Dorcas's daughter, was not moved with the rest of her family to Evergreen Cemetery. It's likely that she is still interred at the site of the old family cemetery.

50

DOVER CENTER CEMETERY

ST. JOHN'S EPISCOPAL CHURCHYARD

Lat 41°27'03.881" N, long 81°55'16.072" W
41.451078, -81.921131
Status: Strictly Off Limits!

Located on the west side of Dover Center Road behind the third house north of Center Ridge Road sits what was once known as the Dover Center Cemetery. Forgotten and abandoned for more than a century, this graveyard was the primary burial site of the Smith and Lilly families.

Sylvanus, Abner and Jonathan Smith were born in Chatham, Middlesex County, Connecticut, to Jonathan and Anna Chipman Smith. All three brothers were active during the American Revolution; Sylvanus and Jonathan served in the army, while Abner enlisted with the navy. Sylvanus started his military career as a minuteman and was present with John Crosier and Jasher Taylor at Lexington Green on the morning of April 19, 1775. He soon became a lieutenant and finished his career in 1782 as a quartermaster's sergeant. Following the war, the Smith family relocated to Ashfield, Hampshire County, Massachusetts, where they made plans for the future.

In June 1811, the Smiths set out from Lee, Massachusetts, and arrived in Dover Township around midsummer. Abner's wife, Rebecca Gibbs Smith, passed away on September 27 of that year and was the first recorded death in the township. Originally buried on Abner's land, she was soon after moved to Lake Side Cemetery in present-day Bay Village and transferred again in later years to Evergreen, where she now rests beside her husband, who died in 1825.

On May 23, 1821, Sylvanus Smith purchased a sizable tract of land, 160 acres, from Jedediah and Sarah Crocker. There, he built his home and operated a farm. Sylvanus Smith was the first to settle in what would become the community of Dover Center. He held this land until March 1827, when he sold the northerly one hundred acres to his son Clark. The remaining sixty acres were deeded to his other son, Sylvanus Jr., the following September. Reserved from the sale of the northerly section to Clark Smith was half an acre, near the western edge of the tract, which was being used as a burying ground. Sylvanus's granddaughter, sixteen-month-old Emerett Holden, died on October 4, 1826, and was interred on the lot. Most likely, this was also the burial site of Sylvanus's brothers Abner and Jonathan, who died on December 14, 1824. Sylvanus Smith joined them on December 9, 1829, when he died at the age of seventy-four.

Just a few months before Sylvanus Smith's death, the Lilly family, longtime friends of the Smiths, arrived in Dover Township from Ashfield, Massachusetts. Brothers Albinus, Austin, Jesse and Bethuel Lilly were instrumental in the founding of St. John's Episcopal Church of Dover in 1837. While searching for a site to build their church, tragedy struck the Lilly family on the afternoon of March 1, 1839. That morning, Albinus Lilly had purchased a cow from a man in East Rockport. After returning home with her, she had managed to get loose and wandered away. Suspecting that she'd returned to her former owner, Albinus Lilly tracked the cow to the Rocky River, where he suspected she had crossed near a milldam. Close by, he located a dugout canoe and attempted to cross the river. The boat capsized in the current, and Albinus drowned. Four weeks passed before his body was finally located about a mile downstream in a pile of driftwood. His remains were returned to Dover, and he was laid to rest in the small burial ground on Clark Smith's farm.

A decision was reached almost immediately. St. John's Episcopal Church would be built near the site of the cemetery. On April 10 of that year, Clark Smith sold half an acre to the vestrymen of St. John's Church. This small tract rested between the half-acre cemetery lot and Dover Center Road.

The cemetery received two more interments that year: Austin Lilly's sixteen-year-old daughter, Florana, and Clark Smith's brother-in-law Rial Holden. Two of Florana's infant siblings had been buried there between 1834 and 1836. Her father joined her in 1848 and her mother, Roxana Sears Lilly, twenty years after that.

Unfortunately, St. John's Episcopal Church of Dover was relatively short-lived. Through the 1840s, attendance began to dwindle. By 1850, the congregation disbanded, and the church was abandoned.

The last two confirmed burials in the Dover Center Cemetery occurred in 1872 and 1875. The first of these was Evelina Lilly, a daughter of Austin's son Albertus, who died at the age of fifteen. The second was William W. Barnes, Albertus Lilly's brother-in-law.

On January 13, 1875, Clark Smith sold his property to his son Henry. The following April, Henry B. Smith sold one acre of this land to Calvin Pease. This tract represented the land formerly owned by St. John's Episcopal Church and the majority of the land previously reserved as a burying ground. It appeared that an entire half acre was not needed for this purpose, and the actual amount of land actively making up the burial ground was sixteen-one-hundredths of an acre. This section, set at the northeast corner of the lot, was withheld from the sale. For a few years, Pease used the old church building as a barn before replacing the structure with a home, which still stands on the front of this lot today.

Sadly, Henry Smith knew the luxury of owning the family farm for only a year and a half, as he died in July 1876. His father followed him to the grave the year after. It is possible that Clark Smith and his family were buried there as well, but the records for Evergreen Cemetery, where the Smith family now takes their repose, do not give a date of reburial.

Following the deaths of Henry and Clark Smith, possession of the farm fell to Henry's only surviving heir, his half sister Betsy. On October 3, 1902, Betsy Smith sold the previously withheld sixteen-one-hundredths of an acre to Calvin Pease, explaining in the title transfer that the land, which had been reserved for family burying purposes, had since been abandoned. Most likely, the graves that could be located were removed to Evergreen Cemetery a year or two earlier.

Today, the exact site of the old Dover Center Cemetery now rests at the northeast corner of the property mentioned above. It sits between the back of a garage and the west bank of Cahoon Creek. Since this former burial ground is entirely on private property, it is strictly off limits to the public.

51

JOHN MACK CEMETERY

A WEST SIDE NEIGHBORHOOD

Lat 41°25'45.760" N, long 81°46'09.883" W
41.429378, -81.769412
Status: Partially Accessible

Johannes (John) Mack was born on February 15, 1811, in Ludwigsburg, Baden-Wuerttemburg, Germany. He met and married his wife, Rachel Minier, in Pennsylvania. They had five sons (four of whom died in infancy) and a daughter.

John Mack purchased his 52.144-acre farm on the German Settlement Road (now West 130th Street) in Rockport Township on December 4, 1849, from the State of Connecticut. Mack operated a farm and a cooperage on this land. John Mack's surviving grandchildren sold the farm to James Cogswell in 1901. In the title transfer, there is no mention of a cemetery, though it appears on a map from 1874 as being on the southeast corner of his property.

John Mack also owned the land that now contains God's Acre Cemetery, also called Immanuel Evangelical Cemetery (established by 1851, according to the title transfer from his father, Matthias Mack). Burials on the southeast corner of the John Mack farm were probably those of his and Rachel's sons who died in infancy and neighbors who had passed away before the establishment of God's Acre Cemetery, where John and his wife are buried.

Currently, the site of the old John Mack Cemetery exists along the eastern edge of the properties that rest between the ends of McGowan and Erwin

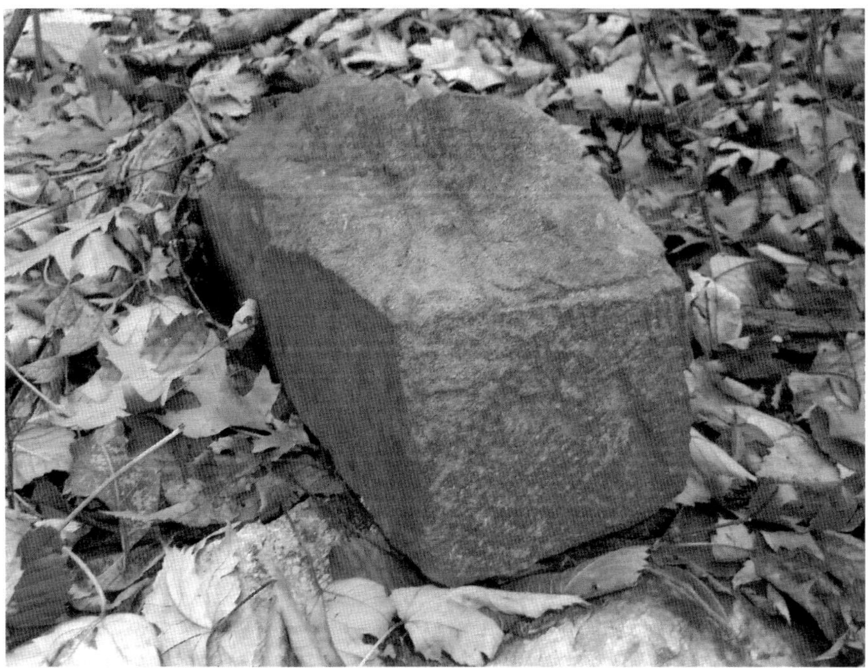

Broken headstone fragments litter the forest floor in the woods between McGowan and Erwin Avenues in Cleveland. *Author's collection.*

Avenues in Cleveland. The majority of it once sat on the last lot on the northerly side of McGowan, while the balance lay just to the north of the fence. During the late 1920s through the early 1940s, both locations were obliterated when a residential neighborhood was built on the site. Developers must have recognized the site for what it was, as no house was ever erected on the McGowan side of the lot. The area that rests on Erwin Avenue now sits in the backyard of a residence. The only part of the cemetery that was left primarily undisturbed now exists along the verge of the woods between these two streets. There, you can discover quite a few pieces of hand-quarried sandstone resting among a telltale patch of creeping myrtle.

It's hard to say exactly what became of the burials that were in this cemetery. Most likely, they're still there. It's possible that many of the tombstones have tipped over and sank beneath the dirt, but those that were standing at the time of residential construction might have been destroyed and discarded. While the majority of the cemetery site is strictly off limits, the area in the woods is accessible. Though some stone fragments remain, the epitaphs are long gone, so there really is no way of knowing who is buried there.

52
CUTTING CEMETERY

ANSEL YOUNG FAMILY PLOT

Lat 41°26'04.855" N, long 81°41'05.985" W
41.434682, -81.684996
Status: Fully Accessible

What was once the Cutting Cemetery is located at the northwest corner of Jennings and Spring Roads in Cleveland. It was so named due to the fact that it sat on a farm belonging to Milton and Maggie Cutting. In actuality, no members of the Cutting family were ever interred there. Prior to the Cutting ownership, it had belonged to the Albert Ingham family for nearly half a century.

Though there are no records of this cemetery, and no evidence of its existence remains, it is suspected that two of the burials were those of a son and a daughter of Ansel Young and Elizabeth Brainard, who came to Ohio from Connecticut around 1819. The Youngs were the first to settle on the land and occupied it from 1827 to 1836. From then on, it was simply known as the Old Ansel Young Place. It should be noted that this is not the same Ansel Young who was the prominent astronomer living on the east side of Cleveland.

Following the sale of the property, the Youngs relocated to Lorain County and are now buried at Fields Cemetery in North Ridgeville. The site of the Cutting Cemetery is now under the sidewalk at the northwest corner of Jennings and Spring. The Jennings Commons Apartments occupy the rest of the Old Ansel Young Place.

53
CLEVELAND PEST HOUSE BURIAL GROUND

A CEMETERY WITHIN A CEMETERY

Lat 41°26'51.781" N, long 81°44'4.588" W
41.447717, -81.742941
Status: Accessible with Caution

The Cleveland City Pest House, a contagious disease hospital, was once located on the southern edge of what is now West Park Cemetery on Ridge Road. This wasn't the first such hospital owned by the city, and it certainly wasn't the last. Urban legends have circulated that this was once a hospital where doctors conducted secret experiments on patients, but this was definitely not the case.

It was originally built as a two-story brick farmhouse and winery by brothers Christoph and Captain Frederick Silberg on what was then called Shunpike Road. It was a fairly large tract of land, consisting of sixty-one acres. Prior to the winery, which was the largest in the area, Christoph operated the Cuyahoga House, a boardinghouse on the west side of the flats. This was in 1845. Frederick, meanwhile, was an organizer of the German City Guard.

On July 22, 1872, Frederick and Christoph Silberg—and their respective wives, Wilhelmine and Catherine—sold the farm to the City of Cleveland for $30,000 to be used as a pest house. The new hospital was finally opened in 1876 to much opposition by neighbors, who didn't want an infectious disease hospital in the area. As with most hospitals of the day, this one had a small cemetery on the premises.

The Cleveland City Pest House operated at this location for just over twenty years before it closed in 1898. Patients were then transferred to a new pest house at the Cleveland City Infirmary on Scranton Road. At its closing, all of the doors and windows were removed from the old pest house building, and the structure was burned down by the city in June of that year.

Bricks from the old building were to be used in the foundations of other new structures but were instead knocked down the hillside to the south,

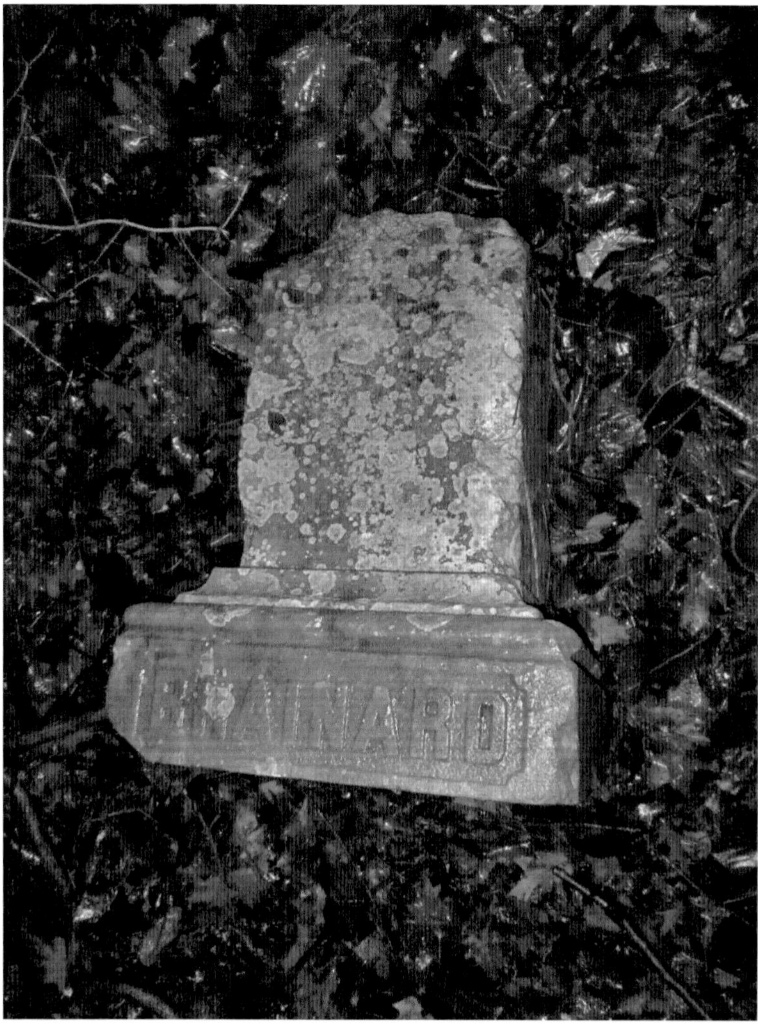

A limestone monument, bearing only the name "Brainard," now lies prostrate in the woods just to the south of section 20 in West Park Cemetery. *Author's collection.*

where they remain to this day. The rest of the land was cleared in 1899 and was opened as West Park Cemetery the following year.

The remains of the old pest house are scattered about the forest floor in the shallow drop to the south of the cemetery. A solitary headstone that bears the name "Brainard" lies on its side just to the west of these ruins. This is all that remains of the old pest house cemetery. It is not a tombstone that has fallen into woods from the cemetery above, as is the case with the headstone of Louise Anderson, which sits about one hundred feet east. The cemetery records are complete, and there are no Brainards buried in West Park Cemetery. It is unknown exactly which Brainard is buried here, as the epitaph is lying facedown. There may be other tombstones in the area, but they are hard to find among the brush.

You should exercise caution when visiting this site. To begin with, visiting should be done only during West Park Cemetery's regular operating hours. Aside from that, the terrain is quite uneven, and some vegetation, such as poison ivy and thorn bushes, pose a hazard. Furthermore, the area is infested with ticks. A suggested time of the year to visit this site would be in winter when there is very little or no snow on the ground. Also, please be respectful of your surroundings. This is an active city cemetery, and there might be a funeral in progress.

54

CLEVELAND CITY INFIRMARY GRAVEYARD

A SAD FATE FOR A PAUPER'S CEMETERY

Lat 41°27'45.673" N, long 81°41'42.201" W
41.462687, -81.695056
Status: Fully Accessible

As stated earlier, it wasn't uncommon for medical facilities to have their own cemeteries. Even a few medical schools had their own places of interment. Granted, most of these held the buried remains from medical dissections. Two such burial grounds were discovered in the very heart of downtown Cleveland. One was the Cleveland Medical College, which was the forerunner of the Western Reserve University Medical College, today's University Hospital. This was located on the southeast corner of St. Clair Avenue and East 9th Street and today is the northern plaza of One Cleveland Center. Several bones, left over from the dissection tables, were unearthed there in June 1885 while construction workers were excavating for the foundation of a new college building.

The Homeopathic Hospital College once stood on the northwest corner of Prospect Avenue and Oak Place, now East 8th Street. This institution was affiliated with the Cleveland Homeopathic Hospital Society, which was located around the corner on Huron Avenue. In April 1894, while erecting a commercial block on the former site of the hospital, employees of the Curtis & Ambler Construction Company unearthed several human bones, as well as a complete skeleton. A medical student collected most of the bones, but those that remained were unceremoniously dumped down the embankment on Broadway Avenue into the Cuyahoga River flats.

Still, no story comes close to rivaling the lack of respect that was shown for those buried in the graveyard at the Cleveland City Infirmary. This medical facility was established in 1855 following the closing of the city hospital that once sat at the eastern end of Erie Street Cemetery. It was primarily a care facility for the poor, mentally ill, aged and handicapped. Deaths there were commonplace, and while those who hailed from well-to-do families were buried in family lots in area cemeteries, the poor were interred in a graveyard on the infirmary grounds.

The burial ground was located on a bluff overlooking the Cuyahoga River Valley and ran down the hillside behind the infirmary toward the river. Graves here were laid out in neat rows and contained wooden grave markers with names and dates painted on them. Among these markers were two marble headstones. One was for a man named Frederick Stephens, which was set by his wife, and the other was for a woman named Susan Harris. Both died in the 1860s.

In May 1886, it was brought to the attention of the Cleveland City Council that the infirmary graveyard had fallen into a state of neglect. Nearly half a dozen skeletons lay exposed above the ground. Many skulls and shinbones were lying loose, and a few coffins had been haphazardly tossed about. People passing below on Jennings Avenue could see, to their disgust, bodies lying on the hillside. Some of the skulls still had hair on them. Blame fell on the infirmary directors, and the Cleveland City Council passed a resolution to prevent any further mistreatment of human remains at the City Infirmary Cemetery. Thus, the infirmary was ordered to properly bury the dead.

Though the infirmary had cleaned up its act, so to speak, the sanctity of eternal rest was about to be undone. In August 1893, laborers grading Valentine Avenue just to the north of the infirmary grounds uncovered many bones just a few feet below the level of the new street. The workers were confused about why they found this until an older resident of the area recalled that there had been a cemetery on the grounds of the hospital. The spectacle attracted many curiosity seekers. Among these bones were random parts that had been placed in a small box, likely left over from medical dissections.

In June 1901, workers again uncovered another section of the old burial ground while beginning construction on a new city pest house. Two years later, this building would become the tuberculosis sanitarium. After reporting the discovery to their supervisors and hospital officials, the construction workers were ordered to continue with the work, regardless of what they dug up. Bodies and coffins were simply tossed to the side with the rest of the dirt

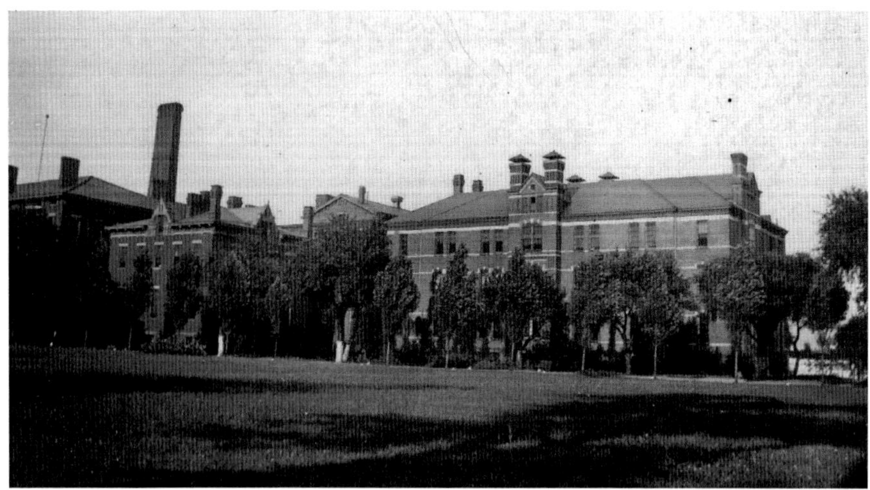

Cleveland City Infirmary, circa 1901. *Cleveland Public Library.*

they excavated. This attracted a group of local boys, who made a ghoulish game of tossing the skulls around like footballs. Physicians and students at the infirmary soon heard about the discovery and enlisted the help of these boys to gather up as many bones as they could. One would think that these medical professionals would have had the respect to give these remains a proper reburial, but that was not the case. The collected bones were strung together as complete skeletons for medical study. Most of the bones weren't suitable for this because of decay and decomposition. Rather than having the bones reburied in an area cemetery, they were simply discarded.

Today, the old cemetery site is under the back parking lot of the MetroHealth Medical Center. Its exact location is at the eastern end of the lot at the end of Metro Health Drive behind the hospital. The only two excavations that have been done on these grounds were the grading of Valentine Avenue at the north end and the construction of the pest house at the southern end. There is a lot of space between these two locations and, therefore, there's likely to be a great deal of human remains still located beneath the site.

BIBLIOGRAPHY

Acts of the State of Ohio. Vol. 77. N.p.: N. Wills, 1880.

Basalt, Hatch & Co. *Atlas of Cuyahoga County Outside Cleveland*. Cleveland, OH: Basalt, Hatch & Company, 1903.

Birth, Bessie E., and Valley View Village Founders' Day Historical Committee. *Valley View*. Valley View, OH: Bessie E. Birth, 1969.

Blackmore, Harris H., and Ferd Mayer's Lithography. *Map of Cuyahoga County, Ohio*. Cleveland, OH: Stoddard & Everett, 1852.

Butler, Margaret Manor. *The Lakewood Story*. New York: Stratford House, 1949.

Coates, William R. *A History of Cuyahoga County and the City of Cleveland*. Chicago: American Historical Society, 1924.

Courey, Bruce M. *Strongsville*. Charleston, SC: Arcadia Publishing, 2006.

Daughters of the American Revolution (Ohio). *The Official Roster of the Soldiers of the American Revolution Buried in the State of Ohio*. Columbus, OH: F.J. Heer Printing Company, 1929–59.

Daughters of the American Revolution, Lakewood Chapter (Lakewood, OH). *Cuyahoga County, Ohio Cemetery Inscriptions*. Cleveland, OH: The Chapter, 1978.

Drake, DeLoss F. *History of Mill Stream Run*. Strongsville, OH: Strongsville Historical Society, 1977.

George F. Cram Company. *Atlas of Cuyahoga County and the City of Cleveland, Ohio*. Chicago: Geo. F. Cram & Company, 1892.

Gresser, John A. *Burials and Removals Erie Street Cemetery, 1840–1918*. Cleveland, OH, 1919.

Hopkins, Griffith Morgan and Company. *City Atlas of Cleveland, Ohio: From Official Records, Private Plans and Actual Surveys*. Philadelphia: G.M. Hopkins, 1881.

———. *Plat Book of Cuyahoga County, Ohio, Complete in One Volume: From Official Records, Private Plans and Actual Surveys*. Philadelphia: G.M. Hopkins Company, 1920.

———. *Plat Book of the City of Cleveland, Ohio and Suburbs, Complete in Two Volumes: From Official Records, Private Plans and Actual Surveys*. Philadelphia: G.M. Hopkins Co., 1912–14.

BIBLIOGRAPHY

Hopkins, Griffith Morgan, Jr., and S.H. Mathews. *Map of Cuyahoga County, Ohio: From Actual Surveys & County Records, Under the Supervision of G.M. Hopkins Jr. C.E.* Philadelphia: S.H. Mathews, 1858.

Hull, Robert C. *Lakewood: Growing Up There*. Bay Village, OH: Bob Hull Books, 1994.

Johnson, Crisfield. *History of Cuyahoga County, Ohio: In Three Parts, with Portraits and Biographical Sketches of its Prominent Men and Pioneers*. Cleveland, OH: Greater Cleveland Genealogical Society, 1879.

Keidel, Helen, and Kiwanis Club of Richmond Heights. *History of Richmond Heights*. Richmond Heights, OH, 1967.

Kelly, Samuel J. *History of Saint Paul's Protestant Episcopal Church in the City of East Cleveland, Once the Hamlet of Collamer, and Originally Known as Euclid, Cuyahoga County, Ohio*. East Cleveland, OH: 1945.

Korenko, Leslie. *Kelleys Island: The Courageous, Poignant & Often Quirky Lives of Island Pioneers, 1810–1861*. N.p.: Wine Press, 2009.

Lake, D.J. *Atlas of Cuyahoga County, Ohio: From Actual Surveys by and Under the Directions of D.J. Lake, C.E.* Philadelphia: Titus, Simmons & Titus, 1874.

Larick, Roy, Bob Gibbons and Edward Siplock. *Euclid Creek*. Charleston, SC: Arcadia Publishing, 2005.

North Royalton Historical Society. *The History of North Royalton, 1811–1991*. North Royalton, OH: North Royalton Historical Society, 1992.

Southwest Cuyahoga Chapter Ohio Genealogical Society. *Memories in Stone: Strongsville Cemetery Book—Strongsville, Cuyahoga Co., Ohio.* N.p.: Southwest Cuyahoga Chapter Ohio Genealogical Society, 1995.

Strongsville Historical Society. *History of Strongsville: Cuyahoga County, Ohio*. Strongsville, OH: Strongsville Historical Society, 1967.

Troutman, K. Roger, Lolita Thayer Guthrie and Ohio Genealogical Society. *Ohio Cemeteries, 1803–2003*. N.p.: Ohio Genealogical Society, 2003.

Van Tassel, David D., and John J. Grabowski, eds. *The Encyclopedia of Cleveland History*. Bloomington: Indiana University Press in association with Case Western Reserve University and the Western Reserve Historical Society, 1996.

Vigil, Vicki Blum. *Cemeteries of Northeast Ohio: Stones, Symbols & Stories*. Cleveland, OH: Gray & Company, 2007.

West, Nancy Fogel. *To Dwell With Fellow Clay: The Story of East Cleveland Township Cemetery*. Bloomington, IN: AuthorHouse, 2007.

Western Reserve Historical Society. *Cuyahoga County Cemetery Inscriptions*. N.p.: Western Reserve Historical Society, 1934.

———. *Reference Guide to Cuyahoga County, Ohio Cemeteries.* CD-Rom 230. N.p.: Western Reserve Historical Society, 2001.

Whittlesey, Charles. *Early History of Cleveland with Biographical Notices of the Pioneers and Surveyors*. Cleveland, OH: Higgins, 1867.

Wickham, Gertrude Van Rensselaer. *Pioneer Families of Cleveland, 1796–1840*. Cleveland, OH: Evangelical, 1914.

Workman, Jeanne Britton. *Pioneers of Westlake, Ohio: Settlers in 1820 and Their Families: Bicentennial, 1811–2011*. N.p.: J.B. Workman, 2010.

NEWSPAPER SOURCES

Cleveland City Infirmary Graveyard

Cleveland Leader, June 13, 1885; May 27, 1894

(Cleveland) Plain Dealer, July 30, 1875; May 25, 1886; August 16, 1893; April 20, 1894; June 2, 1901

Doan's Corners Cemetery

Cleveland Leader, May 19, 1883; June 21, 1891, July 30, 1896; October 17, 1896; September 3, 1898

(Cleveland) Plain Dealer, November 9, 1895; October 6, 1904; September 18, 1907; October 19, 1930; February 7, 1939; October 29, 1943; December 11, 1943; December 23, 1943; December 24, 1943; November 30, 1976

Dover Center Cemetery

Cleveland Leader, March 30, 1896

Erie Street Cemetery (Partial)

Cleveland Leader, August 1, 1884; September 20, 1884; September 30, 1884; May 25, 1897; September 22, 1903; October 18, 1912

(Cleveland) Plain Dealer, August 31, 1901; March 14, 1902; September 11, 1905; October 4, 1905; October 15, 1905; April 5, 1922; December 22, 1925; July 20, 1940

First Rockport Graveyard

Cleveland Leader, November 8, 1858

(Cleveland) Plain Dealer, November 1, 1883; August 2, 1896; September 27, 1940; September 12, 1953

Fosdick/Green Cemetery

(Cleveland) Plain Dealer, February 8, 1960

Gleason/Edwards Cemetery

(Cleveland) Plain Dealer, August 16, 1870; November 30, 1941

Gleeson Homestead Cemetery

Cleveland Leader, February 6, 1877; June 19, 1885

(Cleveland) Plain Dealer, October 11, 1898

Lakewood (OH) Sun Post, February 13, 1992

Hungarian Congregational Church Cemetery

(Cleveland) Plain Dealer, December 9, 1906; February 20, 1907

Lewis Family Cemetery

Cleveland Leader, November 13, 1902

Newburgh Cemetery

Cleveland Leader, December 9, 1881

(Cleveland) Plain Dealer, February 13, 1909

Ohio City Burial Ground

Cleveland Leader, October 2, 1902; February 21, 1903; August 28, 1904

(Cleveland) Plain Dealer, August 11, 1904; August 28, 1904

(New York) Spectator, November 13, 1827

Old Bedford Burying Ground

Canton (OH) Repository, January 12, 1881

(Cleveland) Plain Dealer, October 11, 1951

Old Glenville Cemetery

Cleveland Leader, November 21, 1904

(Cleveland) Plain Dealer, July 17, 1889; October 13, 1889

Old Royalton Burial Ground

(Cleveland) Plain Dealer, May 30, 1963

Ontario Street Graveyard

Cleveland Leader, July 22, 1896

Saint Paul's Protestant Episcopal Churchyard

(Cleveland) Plain Dealer, May 4, 1850

Shaker Graveyard

Cleveland Leader, November 20, 1893

(Cleveland) Plain Dealer, July 13, 1930; October 25, 1961; August 18, 1964; January 22, 1972; August 31, 1975

Silas Johnson Family Cemetery

Canton (OH) Repository, June 4, 1927

(Cleveland) Plain Dealer, June 4, 1927

Sperry Family Plot

Cleveland Herald, March 24, 1847

(Cleveland) Plain Dealer, February 14, 1907; September 23, 1968

The Rockport Tumulus

Cleveland Leader, July 22, 1896

(Cleveland) Plain Dealer, October 24, 1879; August 2, 1896; July 9, 1936

Two Rockport Estates

(Cleveland) Plain Dealer, April 26, 1883

Warrensville Center Cemetery

(Cleveland) Plain Dealer, April 30, 1911; August 25, 1927

Wright Family Cemetery

Cleveland Leader, November 8, 1858; January 22, 1879

(Cleveland) Plain Dealer, September 10, 1860; August 22, 1940; September 30, 1959; April 16, 1975; February 17, 1977

INDEX

Y

ABOUT THE AUTHOR

William G. Krejci was born in Cleveland in 1975 and was raised in the neighboring suburb of Avon Lake. With an interest in local history, he spends much of his time debunking urban legends of Cleveland and works as a seasonal park ranger in Put-in-Bay, Ohio. He is also the author of the Jack Sullivan mystery series and has been a guest speaker at various local historical societies. In his free time, he plays guitar and sings in an Irish band.

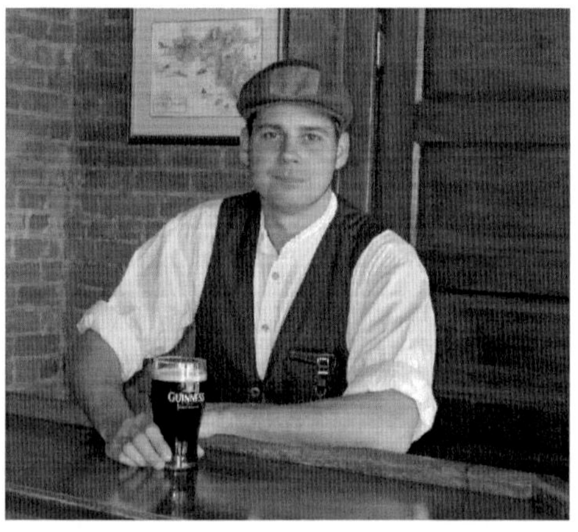

Courtesy of Rebecca E. Haaga.